THE RESTAURANT CAR

A century of railway catering

Geoffrey Kichenside

DAVID & CHARLES
Newton Abbot   London   North Pomfret (VT)

For Paula

British Library Cataloguing in Publication Data

Kichenside, Geoffrey Michael
   The restaurant car.
   1. Railroads — England — Dining-car service — History
   I. Title
   385'.22   TF668

   ISBN 0 7153 7818 X

Library of Congress Catalog Card Number 79–51092

Typeset by
Northern Phototypesetting Company
Bolton Greater Manchester
and printed in Great Britain
by Biddles Ltd., Guildford, Surrey.
for David & Charles (Publishers) Limited
Brunel House Newton Abbot Devon

Published in the United States of America
by David & Charles Inc
North Pomfret Vermont 05053 USA

MENU
(A la carte)

In case of difficulty will passengers please send for the author. Failing satisfaction please write to the Publisher. Our staff have taken every possible care and precaution in the preparation and service of this book but cannot be held responsible for minor accidents of spillage, etc., which may occur on account of excessive movement of the train.

(With apologies to the Pullman Car Co. menu)

67612

INTRODUCTION

Eating on a train can be one of life's most enjoyable experiences, with good food well served and a constantly changing panorama as the scenery unfolds before you. Breakfast with dawn breaking over a misty river valley transcends even the finest paintings in the best known art galleries, while no seascape on canvas could match luncheon in the Cornish Riviera Express as it ran beside the beach between Dawlish and Teignmouth, while dinner in the Midday Scot climbing over the Southern Uplands of Scotland in the falling light evoked far greater memories than any sun-sinking-slowly-in-the-west travelogue. Whether those memories would be of sheer delight, or best forgotten because the soup was cold, the meat tough and under-cooked, or the staff surly can only be answered by each one of us individually, for in the 100 years since the first railway dining car began service in 1879 railway catering has been praised to the highest degree, cursed as the worst in the world and the butt of every music hall comedian. Somewhere within these extremes lies an average, around which about 99 per cent of train catering will fall. Of course some chefs and crews will sparkle with meals and service of distinction, while others will be less than ordinary. That is no different from restaurants world-wide, but on a train the customers have no choice as to whose restaurant they will patronise.

Today, Travellers-Fare, the British Rail subsidiary running the meals on wheels service, is one of the largest catering organisations in the world, with roundly 1,000 branches running the length and breadth of the British Rail network each day, apart from its station buffets. Few land-based restaurants would expect chefs to produce either the quality or quantity in kitchens little bigger than in the normal three-bedroom semi and moreover which are being whirled along at up to 125mph on some routes, constraints taken in their stride by British Rail restaurant car staff. And no restaurant on terra firma would have to hold back the service of dinner because its kitchen and staff were still 30 miles away delayed by operating trouble somewhere up the line which is certainly not the fault of the restaurant car department, or shut up shop altogether because of a hot axlebox. High street restaurants, moreover, bring their staff in to serve the main meal and when it is finished they go home, but railway restaurant car staff cannot leave the train in the middle of a journey.

Over the years designs of railway restaurant cars have changed from the sumptuously decorated first class cars of the 1880s but with primitive equipment, to today's plainly functional but generally more comfortable cars, open to all, many with the latest microwave technology. With higher speeds and much shorter journey times demands have changed, with a swing away from traditional multi-course table d'hôte menus towards quick snacks.

This survey, produced to mark the centenary of railway dining cars, looks at many aspects of railway catering, including the usual and the unusual. Who now can remember having breakfast or supper in a Pullman car on the London Underground? Hopefully this book will revive memories of this and many other services of the past, and highlight the changing needs of the high-speed era.

My thanks are due to many people for help in the supply of material, especially photographs accumulated over many years, particularly from the British Rail regions before their collections of historical material were rounded up for reorganisation, to the staff at the National Railway Museum, York, now the guardians of much of those historical collections and who are making such a splendid job in the restoration and display of full-size relics including a few restaurant and Pullman cars, and to Travellers-Fare for showing me behind the scenes to see just how high-speed meals have added a new dimension to BR's Inter-City 125 high-speed trains.

Totnes, January 1979

GMK

CHAPTER ONE

TWENTY MINUTES' STOP FOR REFRESHMENTS

There was a perceptible, if not too pronounced, lurch as passengers travelling in the six-wheel first class coach running in the 'Scotch' express (always 'Scotch' express in Victorian times) from Kings Cross to Edinburgh felt the train start to slow down when the handbrakes were applied by the brakesmen as the train approached Chaloners Whin Junction, on the southern approach to York. Despite the well-padded seats and backs, the passengers could feel the one-two-three, one-two-three, rhythm of the wheels passing over the frequent rail joints, for the springs, rigidly attached to the coach underframe, hardly absorbed any of the noise and movement of wheel on rail. The compartment was quite small, no more than about 7ft square, which allowed three people to sit side by side facing forward, meeting the eyes of the three passengers facing back on the opposite side of the compartment. The seat cushions were certainly comfortable to sit on and each passenger was divided from his neighbour by an arm and head rest, but the four hours or so since leaving Kings Cross at 10 o'clock were beginning to tell on the passengers for it was a dull, cold day outside and almost as cold inside the coach. There was no heating and the only illumination came from a faint flickering oil lamp in the centre of the roof.

There was no corridor or any means of relieving personal needs, and as the train drew slowly to a stop in York station passengers welcomed the half hour stop. The only problem was that with a complete trainload of passengers, all with the same objectives in mind, one had to choose whether to secure a three- or four-course lunch, to be ordered, eaten, and paid for in about 20 minutes, before or after a visit to the ladies' or gentlemen's rooms. Certainly it was a mad scramble, and the 25 or 30 minute stops by the principal East Coast route expresses between London, Newcastle and Scotland were barely adequate for civilised eating in the midst of a $9\frac{1}{2}$–10 hour journey. But then travel in the 1870s, of which this is a glimpse, could hardly be termed civilised by today's standards.

The development of the British railway system between 1830 and 1870, which had followed the emergence of the self-propelled steam locomotive in the 1820s and 30s, had opened up a completely

Above: The scramble at York in the nineteenth century as a trainload of passengers arrive in the refreshment room, all anxious to obtain something to eat in the short period of the lunch stop. (*Radio Times Hulton Picture Library*).

new way of life for it had become possible to travel from one end of the country to the other in less than a day, even in a matter of hours instead of days or a week or more in pre-railway times. Railways were the great socialisers, for they brought travel to the masses; at the same time they were the great dividers, for they ensured that the masses were kept well apart from the more well-to-do and the wealthy. Labourer should not mix with clerk, nor clerk with lord, and on many routes this was achieved by running the best services only for first and second class passengers, with the third class often relegated to slower trains running in some cases at inconvenient times. The example of the 'Scotch' express of the 1870s, forerunner of the Flying Scotsman, carried only first and second class passengers, although, to be fair, third class carriages were conveyed on a train leaving London 30min later which was only a little slower than the main portion.

Yet one railway, the Midland, stood out like a shining light as an example to the others, although, perhaps, it would be ungenerous to suggest that it had an eye on increasing its share of the traffic by admitting third class passengers to all trains from 1872, and a year or two later by abolishing second class altogether, thus establishing two-class accommodation which gradually characterised British trains right up to the present. Until 1956 the classes were known as first and third, but then became first and second to fall into line with the new two-class accommodation adopted in that year by most railways in Europe.

Although the railways had opened the way for mass travel, by the 1870s there had been little development in passenger amenities — in toilets, heating, and train catering, all of which today we take for granted. On the main trunk routes radiating from London, the longer distance trains to Scotland, Wales and the far South West often

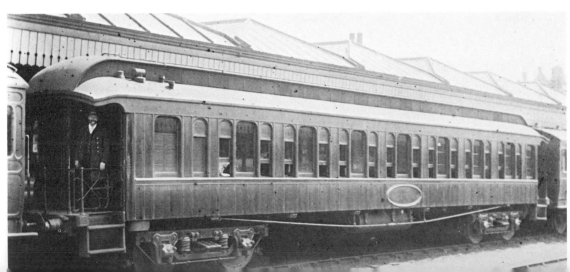

involved journeys of eight to ten hours. Stations designated as refreshment stops were a feature of these longer distance services, with timetables showing halts for dining purposes. On the East Coast route from Kings Cross the usual calling point was York, where in any case locomotives were changed from Great Northern power to a locomotive of the North Eastern Railway or vice-versa. On Midland route services from St Pancras to Carlisle and Scotland Normanton was the dining station, while trains on the West Coast route from Euston to Carlisle, Glasgow or Edinburgh stopped at Preston. Many other stations had refreshment rooms but they were not necessarily designated as dining stations and served passengers boarding or alighting from trains, or changing from main line to branch or cross-country services. Some passengers took a chance on trains calling only for a few minutes by dashing in for a quick cup of tea or coffee, a sandwich or a pork pie, before the train restarted. There were many occasions when a train pulled out of a station with a passenger attempting to get in, holding a cup or glass in one hand and trying to open the door of the moving train with the other, a highly dangerous operation.

On the Great Western all trains between London and the West of England or South Wales called at Swindon for ten minutes for refreshment purposes, one of the terms of the lease by which the Great Western in its early days had conceded to the firm of outside caterers which had been granted the contract for running the station refreshment room there. It was an operating nuisance which the Great Western was later to regret and ten minutes

was certainly not long enough in which to take a full meal. It barely allowed a train load to buy a drink and a snack to take back to their own carriages. Yet this was the only refreshment facility granted even such trains as the Cornishman, principal day service between Paddington and Penzance which arrived at Swindon about $1\frac{1}{2}$hr after leaving London but then took another $7\frac{1}{2}$hr to reach Penzance.

Many passengers of course took their own food and drink with them on the train, not caring to take the chance of not having any food at a refreshment stop or succeeding in buying something but then missing the train. An alternative was to book a luncheon basket, either from the starting station or at an intermediate station en route. The lunch basket was the late Victorian equivalent of today's pre-packed pre-cooked airline tray meal. The contents varied from station to station but were usually not far removed from cold chicken or cold meat and salad, fruit and cake, with a bottle of wine, beer or non-alcoholic beverage to wash it down.

In the United States during the mid-19th century, as railways spread across the Continent train journeys became longer, and distances were far greater than those in Great Britain. Yet the attitude on most American railroads in respect of passenger facilities was similar to that in Britain, although the standard American passenger car was longer than the traditional British carriage and was carried on two pivoted trucks or bogies at each end which gave a much smoother ride. Internally the car was laid out on the open saloon pattern, with seats on each side of a centre passageway leading from the entrance balconies at each end. To improve the rather spartan accommodation on American trains, one George Mortimer Pullman built a novel form of sleeping car with upper and lower berths which was a considerable improvement on anything then running in the USA. He persuaded one of the railway administrations to run the car. The railway concerned collected the ordinary passenger fares and Pullman charged a supplement which he collected from passengers using his sleeping car. From this pioneer beginning in 1858 Pullman sleeping cars became so popular that he had to expand in order to build and operate cars on many routes throughout the USA. The cars themselves had much improved riding, better lighting and self-contained hot water heating systems. A decade later, in 1868, Pullman introduced the first railway dining car in the United States and set the pattern for passenger improvements which spread sooner or later (on some lines or in some countries it was later rather than sooner) to many parts of the world. The initial impetus for the spread of Pullman's ideas to Britain came in 1872 when the general manager of the Midland Railway, James Allport, made a tour of railways in the United States and met George Pullman. As a result the Midland Railway introduced a train of Pullman cars on its service between St Pancras and Bradford in 1874, initiating a Pullman link on railways in Britain which lasted from then until the last tenuous connection of today, the Manchester Pullman running from Euston.

The Midland's Pullman cars, all carried on bogies which gave a much smoother ride than the then standard British four or six wheeler, were of various types but basically consisted of parlour cars for daytime use by first class passengers, laid out as an open saloon with rotating armchairs arranged on each side of the central passageway, and convertible day/night sleeping cars, again generally arranged on the open saloon pattern.

As in the United States, Pullman first class parlour and sleeping cars commanded a supplement for their use. More notable though was the fact that the train was made up entirely of Pullman-built cars, including ordinary first, second and third class accommodation available without supplement, the cars being owned by the Midland Railway itself. The third class seats were arranged in open saloons in the end vehicles which also included a luggage compartment, while the first and second class accommodation was in compartments served by a side corridor leading from the end balconies. All the cars had hot water heating fed from a Baker coke stove, kerosene lamps – a vast improvement over the ordinary rape oil lamps used in conventional British coaches – and toilet facilities, unknown in ordinary British railway carriages at that time, other than saloons and sleepers.

To demonstrate the new Pullman train the Midland Railway and Pullman staged a press run during the spring of 1874 with a trip from St Pancras to Bedford, during which lunch was served to the assembled party, the first occasion on which a full meal was served on a British train to a large number of passengers. A sleeping car in its daytime guise was fitted out with tables, but since no railway vehicles at that time had kitchens it is fairly certain that the meal would have been a sumptuous version of cold meat and salad.

Yet the Pullman type non-supplement cars on the Midland were not a success and were soon taken out of service. Seemingly third class passengers preferred the traditional compartment type coach without heating, toilets and with bad lighting.

Pullman sleepers, however, remained popular, despite such disadvantages as passengers dressing and undressing in bed, since that was the only place they could obtain privacy behind the curtains round the berths. When the new route across the Pennines from Settle to Carlisle was opened in 1876 the Midland extended its Pullman sleeping cars and daytime first class parlour cars from London to Glasgow. In the latter part of the 1870s parlour and sleeping cars also ran on one or two services on the East Coast main line from Kings Cross to Manchester (daytime) and Scotland (night time).

The introduction of Pullman cars to the British railway scene of the mid-1870s was important not because it brought immediate improvements to all railways but it showed what could be done in the way of higher standards in passenger accommodation. That these advances were not immediately adopted by the railway companies themselves was due to many factors, not least the added weight of larger coaches carrying fewer people, which meant an increase in train weight to carry the same number of passengers, over-taxing the small engines of the period. This in turn would have adversely affected the economics of railway operation, and behind railway management there were always shareholders with profit principally in mind. Thus the railway companies themselves did little in the way of extensive innovation if it was going to add to train weight and operating cost.

It was left to Pullman, with his supplementary fares for luxury travel for first class passengers on the few routes for which he had contracts, to introduce other facilities. With the introduction of a Pullman dining car in the United States in the late 1860s it was perhaps inevitable that such a vehicle would be introduced to Britain, but it did not happen until a decade later. The stage was set for the introduction of on-train catering with a special charter train in 1878, consisting of a Pullman sleeper and parlour car and two vans, one of which was fitted out with a kitchen. The train was used on a tour of the Scottish Highlands by a private party. The first regular British dining car came the following year.

CHAPTER TWO

THE FIRST TRAIN MEALS

The first regular railway dining car in which meals were prepared and cooked in a kitchen while running was the Pullman car *Prince of Wales* which, after trials, started daily operation on the Great Northern Railway between Leeds and Kings Cross on 1 November 1879. The car itself was not new, having been built originally in 1875 as a parlour car, named *Ohio*, running between Kings Cross and Manchester. It was rebuilt in 1879 as a dining car with a kitchen at one end equipped with a coal-burning range for cooking hot meals. Seats were provided for 10 diners in the car with a smoking room for nine adjoining, although all seats were used for dining purposes when necessary at peak times. Among the novelties were electric bells by which passengers could call the steward. Although it had open-end balconies, there was no means of passing from one car to another, except possibly another Pullman with similar open balconies, although this was not encouraged, and there was certainly no means of passing to or from ordinary Great Northern coaches. First class passengers wishing to take meals on the train sat in the car for the entire journey.

Initially *Prince of Wales* came up from Leeds at 10am, arriving at Kings Cross four hours later, during which time lunch was served, and it returned from Kings Cross at 5.30pm arriving at Leeds at 10.10pm, with dinner available. The car was owned and run by the Pullman Car Company and passengers were charged 2s 6d ($12\frac{1}{2}$p) Pullman supplement on top of the ordinary first class fare merely to ride in the car, with the cost of the meal on top of that. The Pullman Car Company did not at that time undertake the catering with its own staff which was let out to a private caterer on contract. The car was at first regarded as an experiment but became a permanent feature early in 1880. Five years later it was bought from Pullman by the Great Northern

Above: The first meals to be served on a regular British dining car, the Pullman *Prince of Wales* running on the Great Northern Railway from November 1879. Patronage of the car during its first few months in service was very variable; sometimes the car was full, on other occasions only two or three passengers dined on the way. (*Illustrated London News*).

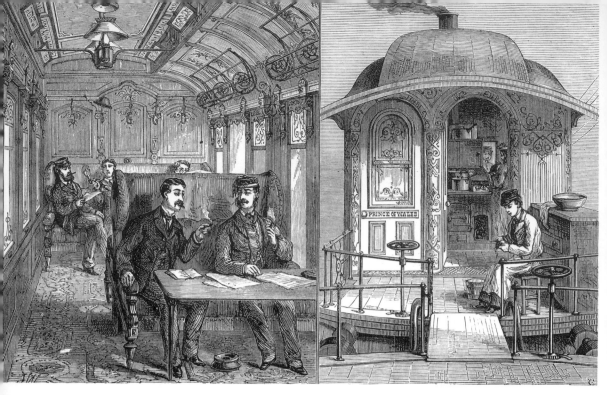

**Sample Patronage of first GN Pullman diner
1879/80
5.30 pm Kings Cross – Leeds**

	No. of passengers		
Date	Intermediate Stations	Leeds	Total
3/12/79	5	13	18
10/12/79	11	3	14
3/1/80	1	1	2
1/3/80	12	5	17

Monthly totals			
Dec 1879	308	Mar 1880	215
Jan 1880	315	April 1880	164
Feb 1880	282		

Note: The number of passengers using the Pullman diner declined when the N. Yorks portion ran separately from the Leeds portion.

Railway and at the same time was rebuilt with gas lighting and cooking.

Despite its success there was no mad rush to introduce dining cars on other railways, but from 1882 the Midland Railway cautiously introduced dining services with a pair of Pullman dining cars on the St Pancras–Manchester route, followed in 1884 by an expansion of services in Midland-owned Pullman cars rebuilt as diners from the original non-supplement cars of the first Pullman train of 1874.

Surprisingly, Pullman diners, whether operated by Pullman or the railway company concerned, were confined to business services between London and the North of England, with a journey time of between four and five hours, rather than the Anglo-Scottish daytime trains which, despite the inclusion of Pullman parlour cars on Midland–Scottish services, still included a half-hour stop for lunch at Normanton during the 1880s. Lunch stops also persisted on the West Coast route from Euston, for the London & North Western Railway would have nothing to do with Pullmans of any sort. Almost a decade after the introduction of the Great Northern Pullman dining car the LNWR started to think about on-train catering but then only on its London–Liverpool/Manchester trains in the late 1880s.

In 1881, after six years' experience of Pullman cars operating singly on its London–Brighton line, the London, Brighton & South Coast Railway introduced the first all-Pullman train in the country – that is a first class only train with supplementary fare – on the Brighton line. It consisted of four cars, one of which had a small pantry and buffet for service of drinks and light refreshments. One car in the formation had electric light, the first railway carriage in the world so equipped. It was powered by accumulators during the journey, recharged on arrival in London from a steam generator. At this time there were various means of lighting trains ranging from the rape oil lamps used since the dawn of railways, and the much brighter kerosene lamps of Pullman cars, to the various forms of gas lighting then becoming established,

Above: The first Pullman dining car *Prince of Wales* introduced to the Great Northern Railway in 1879 and seen here a few years later, after being bought by the GNR and rebuilt with new kitchen equipment and an enclosed vestibule at the kitchen end. (*L&GRP/David & Charles*).

Left: The smoking saloon and kitchen of *Prince of Wales* as placed in service as a dining car in 1879. The car weighed 22 tons, more than 1 ton per passenger, double the rate for ordinary GN first class six wheelers. It would appear that all seats in the car were used for dining on some occasions at times of peak demand. The view of the kitchen end shows *Prince of Wales* coupled to another car with an open end balcony but so far as is known in service it ran on its own. (*Illustrated London News*).

A decade later the London & North Western introduced dining saloons on its Euston—Liverpool/Manchester services. Pairs of dining cars were gangwayed together but not to the rest of the train.

Below is the exterior view of these late 1880s cars and *bottom* is an interior view showing the remarkable patterned ceiling and soft furnishings on the seats. (*Crown copyright, National Railway Museum, York*).

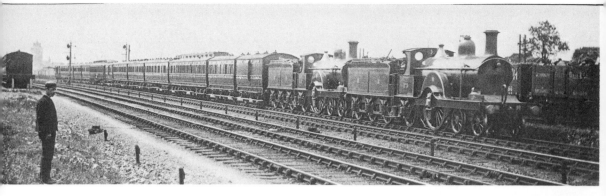

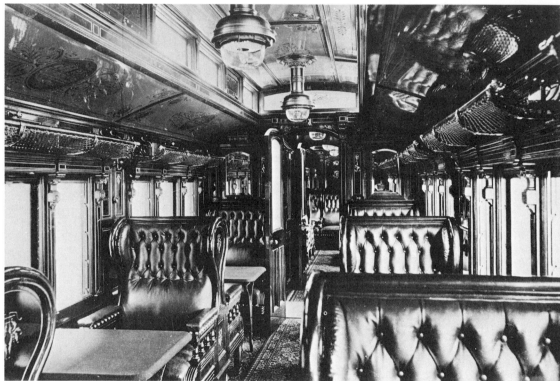

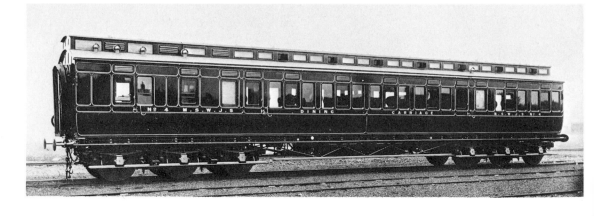

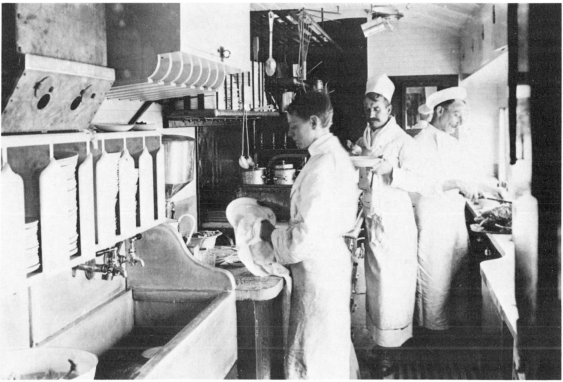

Top left: A Midland Railway express of the late 1890s, including a dining car, third vehicle from the engines, and a Pullman car, distinguished by its domed clerestory roof, further back in the train, which is otherwise entirely made up of non-corridor coaches. (*L&GRP/David & Charles*).

Centre left: Interior view of a Midland Railway first class dining car of 1894 showing the very heavy seats in buttoned leather, and the highly polished ceiling panels picked out with patterns along the edges and in the centre. (*London Midland Region, BR*).

Left: Midland Railway third class dining car built for the Midland Scottish joint stock for through running between London and Glasgow. Normally on Midland dining services in the late 1890s two cars, one first class and one third class were provided for dining accommodation. (*London Midland Region, BR*).

Top: Railway dining car service for all was introduced in 1891 when the Great Eastern Railway placed in service a three-coach dining unit for first and third class passengers on its Harwich–North of England boat train. The number of passengers that could be seated for dining purposes was very small but at least it was a beginning. (*LPC/Ian Allan*).

Above: Interior of a turn of the century Great Eastern kitchen showing the sink and plate racks and in the background the gas stove. (*LPC/Ian Allan*).

The first train on the London & North Western to have dining facilities for all passengers and corridors throughout was the afternoon service between Euston and Glasgow from 1893. It is seen here near Rugby with two dining cars, third and fourth from the engine in the Glasgow portion, and another dining car as eighth coach, in the Edinburgh part of the train. (*Crown copyright, National Railway Museum, York*).

using compressed oil-gas derived from mineral or petroleum oils. The latter type though was a bad fire risk in an accident. Yet despite its dangers coaches with gas lighting were still being built until the 1920s and in a few isolated cases as we shall see later into the 1930s. The last gas-lit coach did not disappear from British Railways until the 1960s, nearly 80 years after Pullman's second experiment with electric lighting in 1889.

Following the success of the all-Pullman train between London and Brighton in 1881 another new set of Pullman cars was built for the service eight years later, all of which were electrically lit, with power generated by a dynamo, belt driven from the axles, carried in a luggage van at one end of the train. More important was the fact that the cars in the Brighton line 1889 Pullman train were equipped with enclosed end vestibules instead of open balconies, with a flexible covered gangway from one car to the next, a feature which had been introduced by Pullman in the United States two years earlier. This meant that it was possible to walk from one car to the next through an enclosed connection; apart from Queen Victoria's twin saloons of 1869 used on royal journeys from Euston to the north, which were the first coaches to have enclosed gangways, the 1889 Pullmans were the first cars for public use to have them. The gangways were more for the use of railway and Pullman staff. One car in the train was fitted with a kitchen and pantry where drinks and refreshments were prepared, but passengers were served at their seats by the Pullman car attendants. With the length of journey to Brighton lasting for little more than one hour it was not practical, nor necessary,

to serve multi-course set main meals. An à la carte menu provided a variety of short meals, for example lamb or mutton chop and vegetables, fish dishes, sandwiches and, of course, afternoon tea.

In 1882 came a development in railway carriage design totally unconnected at that time with railway catering, but which played an important part in the evolution of the long distance train. This was the introduction on the East Coast route of a coach with a side corridor linking passenger compartments with toilets at the coach ends, although without communication from one coach to the next. That development did not come for another seven years with the Brighton line Pullman train just described or ten years on railway-owned coaches.

The last decade of the nineteenth century brought the revolution in passenger facilities and technical advances which began the transformation of the railways from their primitive beginnings towards the modern railway we know today. This period saw the breaking down of almost the last barriers for third class passengers (although it was to be nearly another 30 years before there were such things as third class sleeping cars). There was a general introduction of the longer bogie carriages, compared with the short rigid six-wheelers on nearly all main lines, automatic power brakes were made compulsory on all passenger trains, and heating of trains by steam radiators in compartments fed from a pipe down the train from the locomotive boiler brought the potential for warm trains in winter, at long last signifying the end of that very Victorian passenger amenity – the foot warmer, a sort of metal hot water bottle which passengers could hire at stations.

Leader of the revolution surprisingly was not one of the important northern main lines but the Great Eastern Railway, largely serving East Anglia, which in 1891 placed in service a three-coach dining car set on its Harwich boat train

service from the North of England. The coaches it is true were six-wheelers with very limited accommodation, but not only did they have gangways between the coaches, allowing passengers to walk from the first and second class side corridor coach into the dining saloon, but the vehicle at the opposite end of the kitchen dining car was a third class coach with one compartment laid out for dining purposes, for the first time allowing third class passengers to have hot meals on a moving train. Here was a breakthrough in the social revolution whereby working class travellers could actually eat a proper meal on the journey. This was luxury indeed.

The Great Eastern's pioneering was not lost on the northern companies and two years later the London & North Western and West Coast route, the Midland, and Great Northern and East Coast route trains blossomed forth with first, second and third class dining facilities. Moreover, on the East and West Coast routes at the same time corridor trains were introduced with gangways between coaches so that no longer was it necessary for passengers to travel in the dining car for the entire journey or change into and out of it at an intermediate station. They were not the first corridor trains for that honour goes to the Great Western which placed in service in 1892 a complete train of side corridor coaches with inter-coach gangways on its Paddington–Birkenhead service. In 1893 the Great Western added corridor trains between London and South Wales and London and Penzance. However, the first Great Western corridor trains did not have dining facilities, for the GWR directors were not altogether in favour of providing dining cars, and while the Swindon refreshment room agreement was still in force, there was no point in having a belt and braces operation in respect of train refreshment facilities. Moreover, there was no certainty that railway dining cars would make money, since experience with some of the dining cars on other railways running from the late 1880s had shown that more often than not they hardly broke even and in some cases did not cover the costs of providing meals, let alone maintenance and depreciation of the dining car itself. With competition between railways it was, nevertheless, a case of keeping up with the Jones's, for if one line made an advance in an amenity, a competing route would have to follow suit if it was not to lose traffic.

By 1897 the East Coast route saw the introduction of large 12-wheel coaches for ordinary accommodation and for dining purposes. Moreover, the coaches were built with clerestory roofs sloping down at the coach ends, which visually, made them most impressive vehicles. The clerestory – that is a two-level roof with a centre section standing higher than the sides, containing ventilators and windows, and derived from architectural practice – made its appearance on railways at intervals for about a century from the earliest days until the 1930s. Its heyday really came in the ten years from 1895–1905 when many companies adopted it for all stock, or at least for saloons, diners and sleepers as in the case of the LNWR and West Coast route coaches. The clerestory was certainly an advantage over the low arc roofs of ordinary carriages built until the 1890s and provided a much more spacious airy interior. It was, though, expensive to construct and maintain, and in accidents sometimes formed a weak spot because effectively the back of the coach was broken. The clerestory was also used on Pullman cars from the 1870s until the early years of the present century, but broadly followed the American pattern with the roof sweeping down at the car ends to cover the balconies of the earlier cars. Some railways achieved some fine effects with etched glass designs on clerestory deck lights and in windows of toilet compartments. Often they were beautifully executed patterns or figures, and one or two have fortunately been preserved. By

Above: Although the Great Western Railway was the first in the field with a complete side corridor train in 1892 it was not until four years later that it introduced dining cars, although then only for first class passengers. This is one of the first GWR dining car trains seen around the turn of the century. (*L&GRP/David & Charles*).

Interiors of turn of the century dining cars. *Left* is an East Coast Joint Stock dining saloon of 1896 with two-plus-one seating, individual chairs, wrought iron decoration across the clerestory, and light wicker-work racks for hats. *Below left:* the Great Western Railway preferred to hide its passengers in high-backed screened bays. *Below:* in contrast the London & South Western diners built during the first decade of the present century employed a variety of soft furnishings including floral prints as illustrated here. (*Radio Times Hulton Picture Library: British Railways, WR, Crown copyright, National Railway Museum, York*).

about 1905 railways were beginning to realise that they had plenty of space above the conventional arc roof to the underside of bridges and tunnels which would allow construction of coaches with high semi-elliptical roofs which gave the same spacious interiors, although without the additional centrally-mounted ventilators and windows of the clerestory.

The last years of the 19th century also saw the beginning of the opulence that so characterised the Edwardian years of the new century. In railway carriages this meant in some cases quite ornate interiors with seemingly no expense spared to provide beautiful if fussy, decor, at least in first class coaches. Damasks were used for curtains or blinds, seats were covered in leather, attractive floral printed material, or velvet, walnut, satinwood or other timbers were used for interior panelling, some of which was often skilfully figured or inlaid. Ceilings often had a lincrusta finish with patterns picked out to contrast with the otherwise white background. Brass was used for massive corridor handrails and sometimes in fretted sheet covering heating pipes, while decorative wrought iron was used by some railways for seat frames and luggage racks. This is the sort of setting in which first class passengers dined in style. Third class cars were much less ornate with plain oak or other wood panelling and simpler moquettes.

The introduction of dining cars at long last meant passengers did not have to rush over meals, particularly where they travelled all the way in the dining car. It was thus possible for multi-course set lunches and dinners to be served without risk of indigestion brought on by the mad scramble to get served at the old lunch stops. The sample menu reproduced here was served on the Great Northern Railway dining cars early in 1898 and shows that both table d'hôte and à la carte menus were available. The third class set lunch was similar, but cost only 2s (10p) and was without the grilled turbot. The third class à la carte fish dish consisted of boiled cod and oyster sauce instead of the salmon in the first class car. A noteworthy point was the cost of coffee at 4d a cup, which in relation to the price of the lunch seems quite expensive. By comparison with today's lowest price of £3·35 on the three-course Main Line set lunch menu the charge for coffee in the same ratio would be nearer 55p instead of the actual price of 26p. The first class dinner menu in the 1898 GNR car consisted of a six-course meal excluding coffee at 3s 6d (17½p).

First Class

2s 6d LUNCHEON

MENU

February 14th, 1898

Printanier

Grilled Turbot

Roast Sirloin Beef
Vegetables

Bread and Butter Pudding

Cheese

TO ORDER A LA CARTE

FISH
Salmon Sauce Hollandaise

COLD	FROM THE GRILL
Roast Beef	Mutton Chop
Chicken and Ham	Mutton Cutlets (2)
Roast Lamb	Rump Steak
Roast Mutton	Chicken and Bacon

FRUIT EXTRA

Apple Tart	Crème Caramel

Coffee, per cup, with Luncheon or Dinner extra 4d

GNR menu 1898.

Meals on railway wheels in the first years of the 20th century were becoming a firmly established part of the British railway scene on the main trunk routes. Although railway dining rooms lost some of their trade by the elimination of the lunch stops of long-distance expresses, in practice it was soon made up as traffic gradually built up and services became more intensive and complex. As more people travelled, station refreshment rooms all over the country became mass caterers; without the benefits of modern refrigeration food inevitably had to be supplied fresh and used fairly quickly. The varying traffic levels from day to day made it very difficult to forecast with any accuracy the amount of food that would be needed, and in an endeavour to avoid waste wherever possible, station refreshment rooms were not averse to selling pies, cakes and sandwiches on the next or following day. Glass cake stands were not really airtight and did little to improve keeping qualities. It was little wonder that the railway sandwich of 60 or so years ago gained an unfortunate reputation which has passed into legend, to be drawn on ever since by innumerable music hall and today's television comics so devoid of new material.

CHAPTER THREE

TEA ON THE UNDERGROUND

The great railway revolution really took off in the 14 years from the turn of the century to the outbreak of the first world war. Except for lines running south-east and south from London to the Kent and Sussex coast, corridor trains on long distance services became the norm. Dining cars were added to many expresses and even the Great Western, which had eventually introduced first class dining cars on its South Wales and West of England corridor trains from 1896, shortly after the proprietor of the Swindon refreshment room had been bought out, condescended to provide second and third class dining facilities in some new cars introduced in 1903.

The Great Northern Railway built some trains laid out internally with what became known as open accommodation, that is with a central passageway and seats arranged on each side, either singly or in pairs, in one or two large saloons. In particular quite a number of GN train sets had open third class coaches, particularly those with dining cars. Indeed, the Great Northern established a tradition on the East Coast route by building a number of set formation trains, often quite short and no more than about four coaches, for specific services. One such train, for which two sets were built, was intended for the Kings Cross–Sheffield–Manchester service and consisted of a brake first, a dining car with a central kitchen, 12 first class seats at one end and 18 third class seats at the other, an open third class coach and a side corridor brake third. The coaches were notable in being among the first on the Great Northern to have a high elliptical roof and were also electrically lit.

Indeed, the lighting was remarkably advanced since the lamps in the dining car first class saloon were concealed behind the cornice above the windows so that much of the illumination was reflected from the ceiling, supplemented by table lamps. Electricity was clearly the power of the future for lighting, and a number of specialised vehicles such as saloons and dining cars were equipped in the grand manner with electroliers to provide a touch of the exotic. Gas was also carried on most dining vehicles equipped with kitchens for cooking purposes, since gas stoves were almost standard on nearly all restaurant and dining cars.

There was a subtle different between a dining car and a restaurant car. Press comment at the turn of the century suggested that many passengers might be put off by the more imposingly-styled dining saloons, which implied large formal meals, rather than the term restaurant car, which should be capable of serving anything from a cup of coffee to a snack or a full meal, for passengers of all classes. With this in mind the Great Central Railway on the opening of its new main line to London from Sheffield in 1899 built a number of buffet cars for specified services which ran at times

Below: One of the 12-wheeled restaurant cars built by the Great Northern Railway in 1906 for the Kings Cross–Sheffield service. It contained third and first class accommodation, including such then modern refinements as concealed electric lighting in the first class dining saloon. (*British Railways ER*).

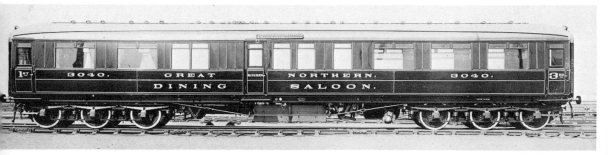

which were not suitable for the service of set lunch or dinner. They were the first railway-owned buffet cars in Britain, although the principle had been seen a decade earlier in the Brighton line Pullmans. The buffet cars were equipped with a kitchen and pantry and a bar counter, together occupying about half the entire length while the remainder of the coach was devoted to three side corridor compartments. Passengers could obtain drinks, à la carte snacks and meals at any time on the journey. Socially, though, the buffet car with bar was not universally liked, for it conjured up visions of the public house, then more associated with working men. Moreover, titled country families from the Shires would have to rub shoulders with heaven knows who, for the buffet car was available to all.

Buffet cars certainly had an advantage in providing a continuous service of snacks and drinks throughout the journey, but on a number of long distance routes the number of passengers requiring meals was growing to an extent that two full coaches were sometimes needed to accommodate diners, with a separate kitchen car where meals were prepared. Among services provided with a high proportion of dining accommodation in pre-first world war years were boat trains between principal inland centres and

Above: From the opening of its London main line in 1899 the Great Central Railway included buffet cars in some of its express services, as for example the second vehicle in this train near Rickmansworth, photographed soon after the turn of the century. (*L&GRP/David & Charles*).

Right: "And what will Madam take for sweet?"; a scene inside an LNWR dining car during lunch, photographed just after the first world war. (*London Midland Region, BR*).

ports connecting either with cross-Channel steamer services or Atlantic liners. The LNWR built an imposing set of coaches in 1907 for its Liverpool boat trains and a year later for its afternoon Anglo-Scottish train. A few years before the Great Western had tried open saloon coaches with a buffet car on its Irish boat trains to Milford but they were not popular.

Yet buffet cars prospered on a number of routes and provided just the sort of service that was

needed on shorter distance journeys. In particular, Pullmans or Pullman-type cars provided the only refreshment services on a number of routes, including one that today would seem highly unlikely. This was, of all places, on one of the London Underground lines, for in 1910 the Metropolitan Railway inaugurated a Pullman car service on a number of trains between its in-town terminals at Aldgate, Liverpool Street or Baker Street, and the Chiltern country towns of Chesham, Amersham, Aylesbury, and the one-time limit of its operation at Verney Junction in the wilds of North Buckinghamshire. Two new Pullman cars were built for the service and for some reason were named *Mayflower* and *Galatea* after the yachts contesting the Americas Cup more than 20 years earlier. Each of the cars seated 19 passengers in pairs of single seats with tables, arranged in three fairly small glass partitioned saloons, with a toilet compartment at one end of the car. At the other was a small kitchen and bar counter and cooking was carried out on a Primus paraffin stove.

Although the two cars were built specially for the service they differed in internal decor, one being panelled in mahogany inlaid with satinwood, with the armchairs upholstered in green and matched by green carpet, while the other car had oak and holly panelling with crimson furnishing. Both cars had doors at the ends of the vestibules which would normally give access to adjacent coaches, but since all other Metropolitan coaches

used on services to Chesham, Amersham and Aylesbury or beyond were of the non-corridor compartment type, there could be no access to the rest of the train and the Pullman car end doors were permanently locked and no covered gangways were fitted. Since Metropolitan journeys were relatively short, lasting from $\frac{3}{4}$hr to about $1\frac{1}{2}$hr passengers wanting meals would need to be in the car for the entire journey.

The two cars were marshalled singly into sets of older Metropolitan compartment coaches hauled by electric locomotives between London and Harrow and by steam locomotives beyond to the country terminus. Thus the cars were fitted with steam and electric heating, and electric light, and were the first electrically-hauled Pullmans in the world. They were booked to run on services generally into London in the early morning peak period, a service each way during lunchtime, and from London in the late afternoon at the end of the working day. There were one or two other workings including the return of one of the late afternoon down services which ran through to Verney Junction, a 2hr journey, coming back at 9.15 in the evening, although patronage could hardly have warranted this train at all. Of more use was the late theatre train leaving Baker Street at 11.35pm serving after-the-show suppers.

Passengers on the Metropolitan Pullmans had to be in possession of first class tickets and orginally paid 6d Pullman supplement for stations between London and Rickmansworth or 1s 0d

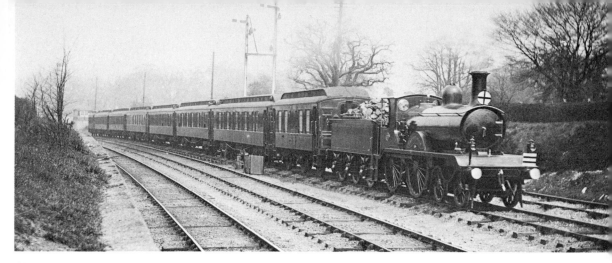

Above: The LBSCR's all-Pullman train of 1889 including the six-wheel vans at each end which generated electricity for train lighting. (*L&GRP/David & Charles*).

Left: One of the two Metropolitan Railway Pullmans which ran on services between London, Chesham, Aylesbury and Verney Junction between 1910 and 1939. At the far end is the bar counter and a small kitchen and pantry, while typical Pullman attention to detail included stands for matchboxes at each table. (*London Transport*).

beyond, later altered to 6d for any distance. Having paid the supplement the passengers were then entitled to use the facilities, including the toilet, even on the underground sections, despite the possibility of a health hazard by discharge into the track ballast in a confined space.

Meanwhile Pullman services had expanded on the London–Brighton line and in 1908 the LBSCR placed in service a new seven-car Pullman train named the Southern Belle. The cars had quite a massive appearance with a high elliptical roof, the first on a British Pullman, and at 63ft 10in long over the end entrance vestibules compared with the 57ft 6in of the Metropolitan cars were quite substantial vehicles and carried on a pair of six-wheel bogies. The train was first class only and seated 219 passengers. The LBSCR had inaugurated an all-Pullman train on Sundays only which completed the 51 miles between Victoria and Brighton in exactly one hour and the new 1908 train extended this facility to a daily service. One car included a buffet so that all passengers on the train could have light refreshments of some sort. Each car was fitted out with distinctive furnishings and fittings and instead of electroliers which clustered lights in the centre of the ceiling the cars had individual lights spread out from centrally placed ceiling fittings, wall lights on the panels between the windows, and the by now traditional Pullman table lamp. Certainly the train reached the highest standard of luxury of any running in Britain at that time. The train was also notable by being the first for Pullman built entirely in Britain, for the cars were constructed by the Metropolitan Carriage & Wagon Company at Lancaster. Until then all Pullman cars running on British railways had been built in America and sent to Britain in kit form where they were erected originally in the Midland Works at Derby, but later in the Pullman Car Company's own works at Preston Park near Brighton. The new train proved so popular that in 1910 its operations were extended to two return workings each day between London and Brighton.

The older Pullmans on the LBSCR continued to run either singly or in pairs on a number of services between London and South Coast destinations. A few had also been used on the London & South Western Railway between Waterloo and Bournemouth or Exeter from the 1890s until about 1910.

By the outbreak of the first world war in 1914 railway catering had become widespread in Britain and took a variety of forms. Although some dining and Pullman services were curtailed during the war many continued. In fact during the war itself one more development took place almost without being noticed, and that was the addition of third class accommodation on the Brighton line Pullmans. Some of the older clerestory roofed cars were rebuilt with seats arranged two-plus-two on each side of the central passageway with tip-up cushions to allow passengers easy access to the window seat. South Londoners must have opened their eyes in amazement, for in contrast to the bumping four-wheelers which could still be found on commuter services from such places as Tulse Hill and New Cross Gate to London Bridge and on weekend excursions, here for an extra 9d (4p) on top of the ordinary third class day fare was a train that they might have dreamed about or read about in books. At long last the mass of day-trippers could travel (almost) like lords.

CHAPTER FOUR

FIRST OR SECOND SITTING?

As train services gradually got back to normal after the first world war restaurant cars and corridor trains continued to expand and set a pattern that was to last basically unchanged for more than 30 years. Indeed, train catering was and still is allied to a large extent to distance and journey time. With the exception of a few specially timed crack expresses, particularly during the 1930s on the East Coast route from Kings Cross and selected services elsewhere, overall train speeds on general express services did not vary to a great extent over the next four decades. By the 1920s Liverpool, Manchester and Leeds were within $3\frac{1}{2}$–4hr from London, Plymouth was just over 4hr away, while Glasgow and Edinburgh were both around 8–$8\frac{1}{2}$hr distant, although this was an artificial timing following an agreement after the 1888 races, eventually abandoned in the early 1930s after which timings came down to 6–$7\frac{1}{2}$hr depending on train and route. Thus depending on time of day and service it was not always possible to utilise dining cars to the full and some were only able to serve one main meal during the journey and on a train leaving say Liverpool around 8.30am breakfast was about all that could be served, since lunch would have been intolerably early with an arrival in London soon after midday. Sometimes dining cars would be taken off part way through the journey, having for example

served breakfast, and then attached to a later train for lunch at a more reasonable time. With an early afternoon arrival in London the train could make a return trip to the north in the evening serving dinner. With some expresses, particularly those to the West of England and to Scotland leaving London within an hour or so of midday, it was not possible to make more than the journey in one direction, returning the following day. Nevertheless, dining cars on such services would probably serve lunch and afternoon tea.

Afternoon tea was almost a ritual in itself for it did not need a full dining car and could be prepared in a pantry and served on trays to compartments, although it was invariably served in restaurant cars running during afternoons. Toasted tea cakes, or toast, assorted sandwiches, bread and butter (Hovis was always available in Pullmans), preserves, cake or biscuits and a pot of tea (Indian or China) was the fairly standard fare all over the country. On some services high tea was available with a grill course supplementing the standard tea menu. Some railways went as far as building coaches specifically designated as tea cars with a kitchen/pantry area little larger than a normal side corridor compartment.

In 1921, the Great Northern introduced a unique five-coach train in which all the coaches were articulated together on six bogies. At one end

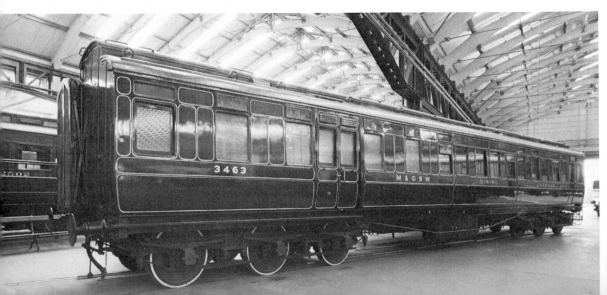

was a third class side-corridor coach including guard's and luggage compartment, then came an open third class dining saloon, kitchen car, an open first class dining saloon, and finally a first class side corridor coach with guard's and luggage compartment. It was intended to run as a complete train but was gangwayed right through so that other coaches could be coupled when required. It ran on the Kings Cross–Leeds service and so sure were the authorities that it would run nowhere else that the legend 'Kings Cross and Leeds' was painted along the roof of each coach.

More important though was the fact that the kitchen car had electric cooking equipment, the first on a British train. The ovens, grills, rings, etc were powered by batteries at intermediate stops but while running from larger than normal dynamos, driven by belts from the axles. When standing at the terminals it was fed by land-line

connection. Electricity having become the standard form of lighting by the 1920s now looked as though it might become established in railway kitchen cars, but railways other than the GNR, and its successor the LNER, were not so convinced.

The grouping of the railways in 1923 from more than 100 smaller companies amidst a few giants into the four principal companies – the LMS, LNER, GWR, and SR – made little difference to railway catering services except to bring some of the former competitors within the same grouping. Midland influence tended to dominate the LMS, Gresley of the GNR continued his policies on the LNER, the Great Western carried on as before, while Pullmans spread their influence on the SR.

At intervals the LNER built new sets of coaches for its principal trains, notably the Flying Scotsman in 1924, 1928 and again in 1938, all of

Above: Afternoon tea was often served in compartments and passengers did not always have to pass down the train to the dining car. This photograph shows one of the large first class lounge compartments in the 1907 LNWR American boat trains which ran between Euston and Liverpool in connection with Atlantic liners.

Left: The Midland Railway by the turn of the century had a reputation for its catering services and during the following years built some handsome dining cars with clerestory roofs, one of which, a kitchen third diner, has been preserved by the National Railway Museum at York. It is in running order and brought out on occasional special runs (*Crown copyright, National Railway Museum, York*).

Right: Many railways provided platform trolleys for refreshment services to passengers on trains without restaurant cars. This is one of the Great Western trolleys selling snack boxes, including sandwiches, cake and fruit, at Paddington in 1921. (*Travellers-Fare*).

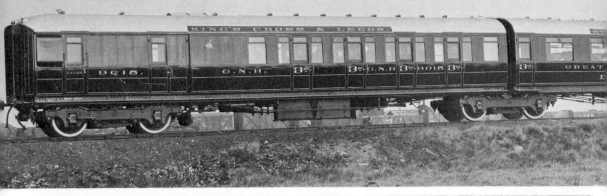

Top: The five-coach Great Northern articulated train built in 1921 for the Kings Cross/Leeds service included a kitchen car in the centre with electrically-powered equipment from axle-driven dynamos and batteries. On one side was a third class dining saloon and on the other a first class vehicle. The inherent disadvantage of this set was that one small fault in any of the vehicles put the entire unit out of action. (*British Railways, ER*).

Below: Christmas lunch on the LNER Flying Scotsman in 1931 with the car decorated, crackers at each table and a menu consisting of traditional Christmas fare. (*Radio Times Hulton Picture Library*).

Above: Notwithstanding the disadvantages of articulation, Gresley on the LNER built large numbers of triplet dining sets formed of a first class restaurant car, third class restaurant car and an all-electric kitchen between. (*British Railways, ER*).

Right: The interior of the 1937 LNER Coronation open first class accommodation with the four-seat alcoves and scalloped shaped tables. Decor showed a break from the traditional timber veneers with partition walls painted in pastel shades and Rexine used as a surface finish. (*British Railways, ER*).

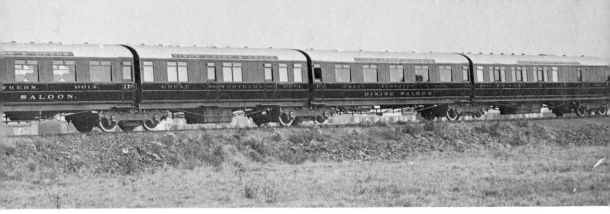

which included a triple dining set, that is three coaches, an open first, kitchen car and open third articulated together. The one problem of articulation was that if any fault occurred in one coach, which might only be a minor thing like a door lock refusing to function, or a sticking brake block, then the whole three-coach unit − or in the case of the five-car 1921 dining set, the entire train − had to be taken out of service. And that resulted in the dining car crew having to transfer cutlery, crockery linen and food to the relief restaurant car− assuming one was available − all because of a fault which might have had nothing to do with the restaurant car.

During the 1930s the LNER introduced a number of special train sets for new high-speed services worked by Gresley's streamlined Pacific-type locomotives. They were usually lighter formations of seven, eight or nine vehicles compared with the much heavier 14 or 15 coach Flying Scotsman train. Externally they were finished in distinctive liveries. Inside traditional timber veneers had given way to painted surfaces or to Rexine finished panels, with pastel shades contrasting with darker colours, on carpets, soft furnishings, partition walls and ceilings. Chromium plated or in later sets aluminium fittings were used for such things as luggage racks. Double-glazed main windows were fitted and the trains had pressure heating and ventilation with sound and heat insulation to reduce external noise inside the coaches.

The original Silver Jubilee train of 1935 for the Kings Cross−Newcastle service had side corridor ordinary accommodation and a triplet dining unit. The Coronation and West Riding trains of 1937 reintroduced the open concept which had tended to disappear from ordinary accommodation on the East Coast route after the first world war. All the accommodation was in open saloons with the third class having two-plus-one seating, but the firsts had a novel arrangement of pairs of single armchairs at a table for two on each side of the centre passageway, partitioned off as four-seat alcoves. This overcame to a certain extent the objections of many passengers to open saloon accommodation by giving some privacy to each group of seats.

Some of the internal design features of the streamlined trains were repeated in other special sets, as for example the Hook Continental where a large number of passengers had to be served with dinner on the outward journey and breakfast on the inward journey to London in the 1hr 20min or so between Liverpool Street and Harwich.

In the early 1930s the LNER undertook experiments in wireless reception relayed to passengers travelling by train. In one train the

COCKTAILS

Absinthe	2'–
Adonis	1'6
Alexander	2'–
Angel's Kiss	2'–
"Atta Boy"	1'6
Barcardi	2'–
Blackthorn	1'6
Brandy	2'–
Bronx	1'6
Chinese	1'6
Chorus Lady	1'6
Clover Club	2'–
Corpse Reviver	2'–
Doctor	2'–
Dubonnet	1'6
Flying Scotsman	1'6
Gimlett	1'6
Gin	1'6
Gin & Vermouth	9d. & 1'–
Hoola-Hoola	2'–
Leave-it-to-me	1'6
Manhattan	1'6
Martini	1'6
Mayfair Special	2'–
Monkey Gland	1'6
Orange Blossom	1'6
Planters	2'–
Side Car	2'–
Tomato Juice	1'6
Vermouth (French or Italian)	9d.
Whisky	1'6
White Lady	2'–

LONG DRINKS

John Collins	2'–
Tom Collins	2'–
Gin Fizz	2'–
Gin Sling	2'–
Golden Fizz	2'–
Pink Fizz	2'–
Egg Nogg	2'–
Horses Neck	2'–

SOURS

Brandy	2'–
Gin	2'–
Whisky	2'–
Rum	2'–

SOFT DRINKS

Lemon Squash	9d.
Orange Squash	9d.
Boston Cooler	1'–
Grenadine Fizz	1'–
Orange Fizz	1'–
Lemon Fizz	1'–
Pussyfoot Fizz	1'–
Grenadine & Soda	9d.

FLIPS

Brandy	2'–
Port	2'–
Gin	2'–
Sherry	2'–
Sherry Cobbler	3'–
Egg Flip	2'6

LIQUEURS

Benedictine	1'6
Chartreuse (Yellow & Green)	1'6
Cointreau	1'6
Cherry Brandy	1'6
Creme-de-Menthe (Green & White)	1'–
Curaco Orange	1'–
Creme-de-Menthe Frappe	1'6
Creme-de-Cacao	1'–
Drambuie	1'–
Grand Marnier	1'6
Kummel	1'–
Port & Starboard	1'6
Stinger	2'–
Silver Streak	2'–

FOR A CHANGE FROM COCKTAILS TRY AN "ABERCORN SHERRY"

Above: The cocktail bar price list of the Flying Scotsman between Kings Cross and Edinburgh in the early 1930s.

dining car of a Kings Cross–Leeds set was equipped with headphones which passengers could hire from the dining car conductor to listen to radio broadcasts. The headphones were linked by cable to the guard's van where the receiver was situated with broadcasts picked up through an aerial mounted along the carriage roof. Passengers could thus have tea and listen to music at the same time. The idea was not expanded and little more was heard of it.

Although the LMS built new coaches for its principal services, particularly the Royal Scot from Euston to Scotland, it did not embark on complete sets of coaches like the LNER, but preferred to introduce batches of the latest stock into its principal services replacing older vehicles which were then passed on to secondary trains. The Royal Scot was equipped with two unusual types of coach in 1928 to help compete against the new LNER Flying Scotsman; one was a first class lounge car with sofas and the other was what was

known as a semi-open first, that is a coach having three side corridor compartments and three bays of open saloon seating. The open section had seats arranged two and one on each side of the passageway but the side corridor compartments seated only four passengers each, thus giving everyone a corner seat so that there could be no arguments. Moreover, the coaches were finished in wood veneers using Empire timbers but each compartment had its own decor. The semi-open first was quite a useful type of vehicle where relatively small numbers of first class passengers were expected because it could be used for both ordinary accommodation and dining purposes. Since the side corridor compartments did not have external doors but had large side windows a table could be fitted into the compartment when necessary to serve meals without too much bother at times of heavy demand.

Both the Royal Scot, and the afternoon service from Euston, the Midday Scot – successor to the

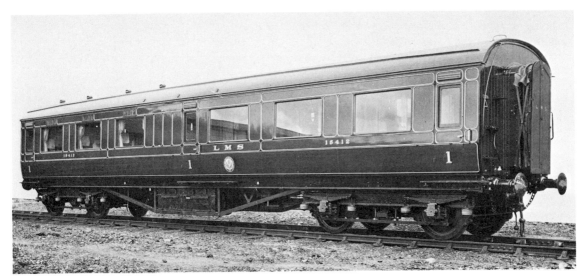

'Corridor', the first corridor train on the West Coast route in 1893 – included portions for both Glasgow and Edinburgh and for many years ran with two sets of dining cars. Indeed, by the mid-1930s no fewer than five passenger vehicles on the Royal Scot were designated for dining purposes, including one of the semi-open firsts just mentioned and two open thirds served from a full kitchen car, and seating 18 first class passengers and 84 thirds in the Glasgow portion, and another semi-open first and open third seating 18 and 42 respectively served from a second kitchen car in the Edinburgh portion. Many LMS expresses and their successors on the London Midland Region until the early 1960s were booked for a full kitchen car serving into at least three open vehicles with the proportion of first and third class accommodation varying according to the demands of the service. The Merseyside Express between Euston and Liverpool, and the Mancunian between Euston and Manchester had such a heavy demand for meals that two vehicles with kitchens were needed on each of those trains. The formations varied slightly over the years but there was usually a full kitchen car serving into two or three open coaches, with a kitchen diner, that is a dining car with a kitchen at one end, serving into another full open vehicle. In some cases the dining car crew operated a 'swing service' in which passengers on one side of the kitchen were one or two courses ahead of those on the other. It meant that the chef could spread the cooking and service of the main course into two groups of 50 or 60 at a time.

The LMS had inherited excellent dining car

Above: One of the LMS luxury semi-open first class coaches used in the Royal Scot and other principal expresses, with part open and part side corridor accommodation. The three first class compartments at the far end each seated only four passengers and everyone had a corner seat. All were distinctively decorated in Jacobean, Chippendale and other styles. (*London Midland Region, BR*).

Below: Normally meals were served in the open saloon accommodation of the coaches illustrated above, although sometimes tables for meals were provided in the individual compartments as here with the service of afternoon tea, photographed in 1928. (*Radio Times Hulton Picture Library*).

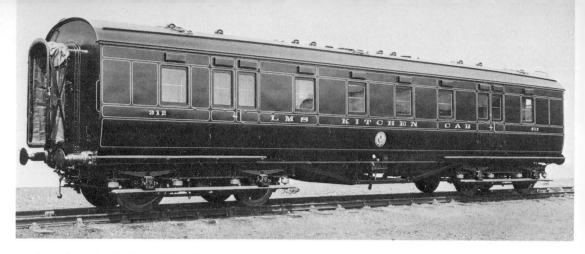

services from both the Midland and London & North Western railways and as we have seen already the Midland continued the practice in which passengers could travel the whole way in a dining car, even after the introduction of corridor trains. The LMS liked this idea and it was possible to reserve seats in the diner for the entire journey on several LMS services, provided of course that the passenger was taking a meal! Part of the dining accommodation was left 'fluid' for casual passengers from other parts of the train. With passengers travelling all the way in the diner it meant that empty seats were not being hauled around and since both the Mancunian and Merseyside expresses loaded very heavily, often in pre-war days to as many as 17 coaches, on a Friday evening, train weight was a vital factor.

Other LMS dining car services generally were provided by pairs of coaches rather like the early days of Midland diners, with the accommodation varying according to the service; sometimes a kitchen third diner would be paired with an open first or open composite coach, or more often a kitchen first diner would be paired with an open third. On these services where the number of dining seats was relatively small in proportion to the total train accommodation, and for fluid seating on other services, two, or sometimes three, sittings of a meal would be provided where time allowed and there was the demand. All LMS-built dining cars containing kitchens were unusual in being lengthy 12-wheelers, 68ft long, looking somewhat massive compared with the normal LMS 57ft or 60ft coaches. Even the most modern LMS dining cars of the 1930s still had cooking by compressed oil gas but with electric lighting; full

The Irish Mail

Breakfast	Luncheon
3/6	**3/6**
Tea — Coffee — Cocoa	Crème Solferino
Horlicks	●
●	Fried Fillet of Cod
Grape Fruit	Remoulade Sauce
or	●
Porridge and Cream	
●	Roast Mutton, Red Currant Jelly
Fried Small Plaice	Savoy
or	Baked and Boiled Potatoes
Kippers	or
●	Sauté of Veal Napolitain
Bacon and Eggs	●
or	
Grilled Mushrooms and Bacon	Manchester Pudding
Tomatoes	or
or	Vanilla Ice
Cold Ham	●
●	
Honey — Jam — Marmalade	Cheese — Salad
●	●
PLAIN BREAKFAST, 2/6	Coffee, per Cup, 4d

Left: Standard LMS kitchen car with gas lighting and cooking equipment, built in large numbers during the 1920s and early 1930s. (*London Midland Region, BR*).

Bottom left: Typical LMS breakfast and luncheon menus of the 1930s; these were from the Irish Mail.

Right: The interior of part of the first class restaurant accommodation of the LMS Coronation Scot train built in 1939 for the publicity tour of North America; it never entered public service in this form, but shows LMS thinking on restaurant car design of that period. (*London Midland Region, BR*).

Below right: During the early 1930s the Great Western Railway was still offering breakfast, lunch, or tea baskets which could be obtained from refreshment rooms at principal stations.

kitchen cars were still being built by the LMS with gas lighting in the mid-1930s.

When the LNER introduced its new Coronation train in 1937 the LMS followed suit with its Coronation Scot, but unlike the LNER train the LMS coaches were not newly built but were adapted from the latest type of existing coach. Interiors were modernised and two kitchen cars were included in the formation to allow the service of a late lunch, afternoon tea and an early dinner to all passengers on the train.

The London & North Eastern introduced a few long-distance Pullman services, most notable of which was the Queen of Scots between Kings Cross, Leeds, Edinburgh and Glasgow, and the Yorkshire Pullman between Kings Cross, Leeds and Bradford, amongst others. The Southern Railway worked very closely with the Pullman Car Company as we shall see in the next chapter, while the Great Western had a short and unsuccessful partnership with Pullmans on the Torquay Pullman between Paddington and Paignton in 1929/30. This train, however, was not a success, partly because it was duplicated very closely by the Great Western's own Torbay Express, available without supplement, and because Great Western catering had by then improved to a standard quite the equal of anything Pullman could do. Great Western train catering philosophy was generally based on the use of a dining car with a smallish kitchen, containing both first and third class accommodation, seating a relatively small number of diners, but at several sittings. Even so both the Torbay Express and the Great Western's other crack train the Cornish Riviera Express between Paddington and Penzance were fairly wasteful of resources because both trains made only a single journey in a day and two sets of coaches were required to make the both ways trips every 24hr. Certainly in the

1930s the West Country was primarily regarded by the GWR as a holiday area and there was little pretence at providing a business service which would give the West Country businessman a quick service to London in the morning, time for calls or meetings during the afternoon and a late return in the evening, such as was afforded to executives from the Midlands and North. For that we had to wait until the 1960s.

Yet Great Western restaurant cars in the 1930s gained a reputation second to none. Countless holidaymakers were fed on their way between London and the West Country holiday resorts although on some trains because of the large number of passengers, with restaurant and buffet cars and crews spread as widely as possible, only a simplified two-course menu with cold meat and

Station Refreshment Rooms

The charges for Breakfast, Luncheon and Tea Baskets are as shewn below:

BREAKFAST BASKETS

Eggs and Bacon (or Cold Ham), Bread, Butter, Preserves,
Tea, Coffee or Cocoa⠀⠀⠀⠀⠀⠀⠀⠀3/6

LUNCHEON OR DINNER BASKETS

Meat (Hot or Cold), (Roast or Pressed Beef, etc.), Bread,
Butter, Cheese, Salad, etc.⠀⠀⠀⠀⠀⠀3/-
Cold Chicken and Ham, Bread, Butter, Cheese, Salad, etc.⠀3/6
Chop or Steak, Bread, Butter, Cheese, etc.⠀⠀⠀3/6

TEA BASKETS

Pot of Tea, Coffee, etc.,
Bread and Butter, Cake
or Bun and Fruit.
Per person⠀⠀1/3

¶ In view of the serious losses by breakage and otherwise of Basket Fittings, the Company venture to solicit the co-operation of passengers to ensure their proper use, and to replace them in the Baskets when finished with.

Restaurant Cars

TARIFF
(Ordinary Trains)

Breakfast (Table d'Hôte)	3/6
Luncheon ditto	2/6 and 3/-
Ditto ditto (Cars on Services operating between the G.W. and L.M.S., L.N.E., and Southern Lines)	3/6
Dinner (Table d'Hôte)	5/-

TEAS.—Pot of Tea or Coffee, with Cut Bread and Butter, per person, 9d.

Full Tea Tariff exhibited in the Restaurant Cars.

N.B.—The charge for Table d'Hôte Luncheon served on the "Cornish Riviera Limited" and "Torbay Limited" Expresses is 4/- per head.

Passengers are requested to note that Dogs are not allowed in the Restaurant Cars.

GENERAL ARRANGEMENTS

RESERVING SEATS.—To secure a seat for breakfast, luncheon or dinner in the restaurant car, it is necessary to obtain a ticket from the Conductor in charge of the car. The seats are numbered to correspond with the numbers printed on the tickets. The attendants will inform passengers when the meals are ready, and conduct them to their seats in the restaurant car. Seats can only be occupied during the time a meal is being served.

RELAYS.—If all the passengers requiring a meal cannot be accommodated at one sitting, further meals will be served if time permit, and tickets for "First," "Second" or "Third" meal issued accordingly. The Company cannot undertake to provide for every passenger in the train.

CORRIDOR COMMUNICATION.—Passengers requiring a meal *en route* should see before starting that access to the Restaurant Car is possible from the compartment in which they propose to travel, as communication throughout the train is not always provided. Passengers travelling in slip coaches cannot obtain access to the Restaurant Cars.

Above: Great Western restaurant car of the pre-first world war period which survived with modernisation to the 1950s. The little extra width of some Great Western coaches is evident in this spacious interior and a detail touch are the vases of flowers at each table. (*LPC/Ian Allan*).

Left, lower: Great Western Railway restaurant car tariff.

salad, and a sweet could be offered. But then on hot summer Saturdays who would want roast joints anyway? On peak summer weekends, the Great Western used to despatch a train of restaurant cars from Paddington to Newton Abbot on Friday evenings ready stocked and staffed to work up trains on the Saturday. The cars were otherwise used on ordinary Monday to Friday trains, some of which did not run or did not need refreshments on Saturdays. The crews lodged overnight at Newton Abbot, sleeping in railway offices or sometimes in the cars themselves. Even in recent years overnight lodging by restaurant car crews lasted long after it had been eliminated on train crew rosters. There was always a snag on certain Great Western trains for passengers travelling in slip coaches — that is the coaches uncoupled at speed to serve intermediate stations while the main part of the train continued non-stop to its first halt miles ahead — there was no access to the restaurant car since the slip coach had no gangway to the main part of the train. For a time, at least one GW slip portion included its own restaurant car. Unfortunately there were just not enough cars and crews to provide refreshments on every train and on many holiday services it was not even possible to get a cup of tea.

CHAPTER FIVE

PULLMANS TO BRIGHTON – BUFFETS TO BOGNOR

Services on the Southern Railway to the Kent and Sussex coasts were an altogether different proposition from those running north from London. Even with steam haulage in the 1920s, Brighton was only 60min away from London, and nearly all other principal South East and South Coast resorts from Dover to Portsmouth were no more than 2hr away, and even Bournemouth only 2½hr by the best train. Thus refreshment services on these routes did not need to be more extensive (and on most routes could not be anyway) than a snack or grill service except on the Bournemouth line. Former London Brighton & South Coast Railway routes were well provided with single Pullman cars in addition to the all-Pullman first and third class Southern Belle to Brighton itself and during the 1920s individual Pullmans were extended to South Eastern services, including Continental boat trains to Dover and Folkestone. In contrast, on the former London & South Western line, although the LSWR had dabbled with Pullmans at various times none had survived to be taken over by the Southern Railway. Ordinary company-owned dining cars were thus used on the longer distance services out of Waterloo to Bournemouth and to the West of England, but with catering contracted out to a hotel group company.

That broadly was the situation until the early 1930s when the Southern started its ambitious programme of main line electrification following conversion of many of its London suburban routes during the previous decade or so. The London–Brighton main line was the first to be electrified, and, following tradition, Pullman cars were included in the new main line electric multiple-unit trains. Unlike the Metropolitan Pullmans which were hauled by electric locomotives, the Brighton line six-coach express sets included motor coaches at each end of the formation with a driver's and guard's compartment at the outer ends of the motor

Right: A feature of many Southern Railway South Coast express electric services from the 1930's was the inclusion of a single Pullman car with both first and third class accommodation, which, although limited, remained popular throughout their existence. (*G. M. Kichenside*).

coaches. Five of the six coaches in each set were generally similar to contemporary Southern Railway ordinary corridor coaches and included both open saloon and side corridor accommodation; one coach within each set was a Pullman car laid out with a complex arrangement of a kitchen and pantry at one end, a first class saloon of eight single seats arranged in pairs on each side of the central passageway, then came a short side corridor past a first class compartment of four seats, a toilet compartment, and finally a third class saloon of 16 seats with seats arranged two-plus-two on each side of the central passageway at tables for four. Although the six-coach trains had gangways between all vehicles within the set there was no bar in the Pullman car so that it was not possible for passengers travelling in the rest of the set to wander through to the Pullman for service. When longer trains were needed two six-coach sets were coupled together but each had its own Pullman car since there was no communication between one set and the other.

Pride of the Brighton line were the three five-car electric trains of all-Pullman stock built for what was still called the Southern Belle, although soon renamed the Brighton Belle. These were the first electric multiple-unit Pullmans in the world. Normally two sets were coupled together to form a ten-car train while the third acted as spare or for maintenance purposes. Each of the five-car Brighton Belle units was composed of a motor

brake parlour car, with 48 seats, at each end, a non-powered third class parlour seating 56, and two kitchen first class cars each seating 20, and refreshment service was available right through the train. Thus when two trains were coupled to form a ten-car unit it included four kitchen cars.

Later units built for the Hastings electrification did not have Pullmans but one coach was fitted up with a pantry for corridor service of refreshments but staffed by a Pullman attendant. With the resulting shuffle of the electric Pullman units the typical Southern South Coast express consisted of one six-car set with a Pullman car coupled to one six-car set including a pantry car, and they worked to various destinations from London to Hastings, Eastbourne, Brighton, Worthing and Littlehampton. In 1938 the last of the LBSCR coastal main lines from Victoria via Horsham was electrified but the new trains provided were woven around a different concept with four-car sets having gangways not only through the set but also at the outer ends. This time though the Southern Railway opted to build its own catering vehicles and included in certain sets a buffet car having a long bar counter with bar stools so that passengers could be served seated at the counter, with tables for four built into the sides just below the windows occupying the remainder of the car. The tables themselves had scalloped edges to allow passengers to sit facing out of the window. Although the cars were railway-owned they were staffed by Pullman attendants and stocked and supplied by the Pullman Car Company.

The menus on the Bognor, Brighton and Hastings lines together with certain other of the Southern's shorter distance Pullman services to the South East were fairly standardised since the electric units were in service all day (with the exception of the Brighton Belle, but even that made three return trips between London and Brighton, starting at 11.00 and arriving back in London at 21.25 for most of its life) with only short turn-rounds at the terminals. A la carte service was

Above: Pride of the Brighton line was the all-electric *Brighton Belle* unit which ran from 1933 until its demise in 1972. (*L&GRP/David & Charles*).

Below: The general Pullman car tariff on Southern Region South Coast express services in 1960, including the Bognor and Hastings buffet cars.

Facing page: The Mid-Sussex Bognor line refreshment cars built for the electrification in 1938 included a buffet counter with partitions and tables having a common scalloped theme. (*Radio Times Hulton Picture Library*).

Tariff

A LA CARTE BREAKFAST
Cereal 1/- Fruit Juices: Pineapple 1/6 Tomato 1/6 Orange 1/6
Eggs Styled to Choice each 1/- Grilled Bacon (portion) 2/-
Grilled Frankfurters or Cambridge Sausage (each) 1/-
Grilled Kippers (Single) 1/6 (Pair) 3/-
Hot Buttered Toast 6d.
Dry Toast & Curled Butter 9d Individual Preserves 6d

SANDWICHES

Ham, Meat and other Centres	1/9

SNACK SERVICE			
Baked Beans on Toast ... 2/-	Toasted Bacon Sandwich	2/6
Sardines on Toast ... 2/-	Welsh Rarebit ...	2/-
Mild Cured Ham (plate) 5/6	Tomato (portion) ...	1/-
French Fried or Whipped Potatoes 1/-		

SUNDRIES

Cut Hovis and White Bread and Butter (two rounds)	6d.
Roll or French Bread ... 3d.	Butter (portion) ...	3d.
Quality Cake ... ... 6d.	Cadbury's Shortcake ...	6d.
Kit Kat Chocolate Biscuits 6d.	Cheese Biscuits (packet)	3d.
Biscuits Sweet (packet)... 6d.	*Assorted Slab Chocolate	6d.
Toasted Teacake ... 6d.	*Smith's Potato Crisps (packet)	4d.
Cheese Wedge ... 9d.	*Smith's Cheddar Sandwich	
* In Buffet Cars Only	(packet)	4d.

● A LA CARTE SERVICE
Hot Soup with Golden Croutons 1/6
Fruit Juices : Pineapple 1/6 Tomato 1/6 Orange 1/6
*The Dish of the Day 8/6
*Cold Collation with Seasonal Salads 8/6
Sweet Course 2/-
Cheese Board 2/-
Coffee 8d.
Bread Basket of Oven Crisp White & Hovis Rolls
Ryvita & Melbex Toast & Curled Butter 6d.
*Price includes Two Styles of Potatoes & Second Vegetable Tray
● Luncheon Timings

Passengers are Respectfully reminded that all items listed upon this Tariff are subject to service availability.

The A.B.C. Railway Guide can be consulted on application to the conductor.

available all day. On suitable services running before mid-morning breakfast was available with the usual grilled bacon and an egg, or sausage, bacon and tomato, or eggs 'styled to choice'. For many years grilled kippers were a feature of Pullman breakfasts for those who preferred fish to bacon, and when in Pullman's last years kippers were removed from the menu regular Pullman passengers, including some well-known stage personalities, created such a rumpus that they were quickly restored.

A number of à la carte main dishes were available, including soup (in Pullman cars invariably garnished with golden croutons), cold meats with salad, and such grills as chops, steaks or Dover sole with vegetables, together with a sweet course and the cheese tray. Then there would be sandwiches plain or toasted, buttered toast, Welsh rarebit, eggs, permutations on afternoon tea or simply a pot of coffee and biscuits. In times of stress or headache the Pullman attendant could always sell you an Aspro or cigarettes. Cigars were specially selected for the Pullman Car Company. Alcoholic beverages were of course available, although the physical size of a Pullman pantry limited the variety that could be offered, and wine was only served on certain services. Aperitifs, spirits, beer, cider and minerals were usually available.

Meanwhile in 1937 the Southern electrified its main line between Waterloo and Portsmouth but here the whole catering concept was traditional with a kitchen serving into first and third class dining saloons, generally offering set meals. Apart from passengers travelling to and from Portsmouth this was part of the route to the Isle of Wight, taking over 3hr to some Island destinations. A la carte dishes were available on certain trains running outside the times of main meal service.

The Southern Railway's other two principal all-Pullman trains became established in the 1930s, although starting a few years earlier, the Bournemouth Belle from Waterloo to Bournemouth which reintroduced Pullmans to the former London & South Western line, and the Golden Arrow Continental boat train between Victoria and Dover. The Arrow formed part of a through London–Paris service and had a Pullman counterpart running in France between Calais and Paris. It was a train with a very chequered history but in the days when flying between London and Paris probably meant a rather uncertain and very

bumpy trip in a rather large bi-plane from the grass field at Croydon airport, a rail and sea journey was the accepted means for practically everyone to go to the Continent. The Golden Arrow provided that added impetus of a luxury service with catering to match, although for much of its life it never seemed to run at quite the right time to serve main meals. An 11.00 departure from London was too early for lunch and on the return in the late afternoon set tea would have been called for, or not even that if the Channel crossing had been rough. Nevertheless the fairly standard Pullman à la carte menu was available enhanced with such items as smoked salmon, either as a dish or in sandwiches, and what was described as 'Assiette Anglaise', a meat platter. Russian tea was also available.

Of all the railways during the 1930s the LNER undoubtedly developed buffet facilities to the greatest extent and, moreover, introduced them on secondary services that had not hitherto had any catering facilities at all. A number of cross-country routes were served by buffets, including Newcastle–Carlisle and Manchester–Cleethorpes, but their greatest use was on shorter distance main line services, as for example Liverpool Street–Clacton and Cambridge, and probably best known of them all, the Kings Cross–Cambridge service via Hitchin, in which short five or six-coach expresses, including a buffet were named as 'Cambridge Buffet Express' and ran at intervals through the day. The cars themselves usually included 24 seats which were unclassified and thus available to first or third class passengers, and a buffet counter with a small kitchen, so that either main courses or other hot snacks or light refreshments could be served as ordered. Buffet

L N E R BUFFET CAR

SPECIAL TEAS

1/6

Choice of—

Boiled Egg.

Veal and Ham or Pork Pie.

Scotch Egg.

———

Bread and Butter.
Cake or Pastry.
Preserves.
Tea.

2/-

Choice of—

Veal and Ham Pie.   Salad.
York Ham   Ox Tongue.
Pressed Beef.

———

Bread,   Butter.
Cake or Pastry.
Preserves.
Tea.

cars were also provided in a number of excursion sets built specifically by the LNER for this form of working and known as tourist stock, with accommodation throughout in open saloons and seats arranged two-plus-two on each side of the central passageway. Some of these trains worked quite long distances to East Coast resorts from London and contrasted with the rather spartan non-corridor coaches often used for excusions on other routes.

The LMS also looked at buffet cars during the 1930s and built one car to try out the idea followed by four more in 1936, but were clearly not convinced of the advantages, probably because most LMS expresses were fairly heavy formations which needed a full restaurant car anyway.

The Great Western also tried out buffet cars on one or two services, in particular a quick lunch car consisting of a kitchen serving a long bar counter extending for much of the length of the rest of the car, with bar stools so that passengers could eat snacks at the counter. The Great Western built several buffet cars after experiments with the conversion of some of the older clerestory-roofed diners into buffets in the early 1930s, but their use was not widespread.

More interesting though was the provision of a small buffet in a single diesel railcar unit which the Great Western introduced in the early 1930s to run between Birmingham and Cardiff. The car was designated as one class, that is third class only, but a small supplement was charged to travel in it and it introduced diesel traction for passenger purposes to a British railway.

The Great Western also built a number of special sets of coaches designated specifically for excursion use but their philosophy was to provide

Above left: Sample tea menu in LNER buffet car which operated on many services not requiring a full restaurant car. There was also a set three-course cold luncheon menu at 2s 6d.

Left: The Great Western also tried buffet cars some in the form of quick lunch counters, one of which is seen here decorated for Christmas in 1934. (*Radio Times Hulton Picture Library*).

a full meal service where necessary rather than a buffet as on the LNER. Despite developments in road transport this was still the era when works' outings were planned round the hire of a complete train from London or Birmigham to South Devon or South Wales. At the other extreme was the Great Western's answer to the Pullman car, with its specially built saloons designed for the Plymouth–London American boat traffic.

Internally they resembled to a large extent contemporary Pullmans and some of the cars were fitted with kitchens so that passengers could be served with meals at their seats. The longer journey from Plymouth to Paddington moreover gave the opportunity to serve something more substantial than would be needed for example on a Pullman car between Southampton and Waterloo on one of the Southern's ocean liner expresses.

CHAPTER SIX

TAVERNS, CAFETERIAS AND SELF-SERVICE

The second world war changed many things in most people's lives but not least in social habits in eating out. Railway dining and Pullman cars had disappeared for the duration and food was rationed so that multi-course meals in general became a thing of the past. 'British Restaurants' and armed services mess rooms introduced practically everyone to self-service, to queueing with tray in hand watching while soup was ladled out in front of you, and plates of meat (if you were lucky) and vegetables enclosed by a metal cover and stacked in a hot cupboard were removed one by one to be served. After the war it was never quite the same again, for less elegant standards and greater demand for quick meals had become part of a way of life. Moreover, self-service was here to stay even if it took a few years before the railways managed to adapt. When restaurant and Pullman cars were restored in the year or two after the war ended, their methods could not be changed immediately since finance was not available for undertaking physical conversions to existing coaches, most of which were without bar counters, so essential for self-service.

The first developments came in 1949 when with more than a blast of publicity fanfare the infant nationalised British Railways tried a gimmick by introducing some new refreshment vehicles styled inside and out to look like an olde worlde British inn. The two-car restaurant buffet sets consisted of a kitchen/tavern car, including a cocktail bar and snack counter, with seats for 12 in oak settles backing the walls at the snackbar end, coupled to a

third and first class dining saloon. Third class seats were arranged conventionally at tables for four though with loose chairs, but the first class half of the car had pairs of seats arranged back to the side walls facing inwards at tables for two. The decor in the cocktail bar and snack counter area of the kitchen car included timbered beams, both across the ceiling and forming vertical panels to represent the oak and whitewash plaster walls of a country tavern. Externally the cars were finished basically in the then new British Railways crimson lake and cream livery but part of the kitchen/tavern car was painted to represent brick below the waist and half timbered whitewashed walls above the waist. All the taverns were named, including *The White Horse, Jolly Tar, Dolphin, Three Plovers, The Bull, The Salutation, The Green Man*, and *The Crown*. There was just one slight problem as far as passengers were concerned, there were very few windows. In the dining saloons they were provided only as sliding ventilators in the upper part of the bodyside so that passengers could not see out while eating or drinking. It was certainly a brave attempt at doing something different and was welcomed in the post-war years for that alone, but it was a gimmick that the travelling public did not like and after a few years, following much criticism, the kitchen buffet cars had windows added and a more conventional layout was adopted for the dining saloon. The cars were notable though for the use of plastic veneers for some partition wall panels since the expansion of the plastics industry during the second world war had produced a material to rival the timber veneer.

Yet it was to be another few years before any further changes were introduced in train catering, largely because of restrictions on capital expenditure and the building of new coaches, allied to a shortage of materials which meant that BR was forced into reconditioning or rebuilding older stock internally. By 1954 self-service made a step forward with the introduction on a number of routes of cafeteria cars converted from older coaches, some of which had been catering vehicles, particularly former LMS kitchen cars. Now they had a relatively small central kitchen bounded on one side with traditional tables for four and on the other by a centrally placed longitudinal table along the length of the car with bar stools on each side. This kept the counter area free of people actually eating, the object being to collect meals on a tray and take them to the seats elsewhere in the car or through the gangway into an adjacent car or to the passenger's own seat. The new cars were equipped to supply normal cold fare, including sandwiches, pork pies, cakes etc, but among the kitchen equipment was a deep freeze in which main courses prepared and cooked at restaurant car depots and then frozen could be kept in a cafeteria car and reheated when required. This meant that the menu could be broadened to include chicken à la king, braised steak or other entrées with vegetables, and the number of courses depended on the passenger's own wishes. He could for example select soup or fruit juice, the main course, a sweet, and cheese and biscuits, or simply the main course and a sweet. By then also bottled gas had become available and was used for ovens or grills on the cafeteria cars. It was safer than oil-gas and more flexible than electricity.

By the mid-1950s BR was beginning to introduce a new range of standard coaches to run in all parts of the country which included several designs of catering vehicle. The first designs tended to follow established practice, for example full kitchen cars serving only formal meals into adjoining open dining saloons, or kitchen diners with a kitchen and seating in the one car. By the end of the 1950s BR had numerous variations on the theme. Some of the dining accommodation was specified for first or second class passengers, while in others it was unclassed. Undoubtedly the most useful of the BR standard catering vehicles and numerically among the largest was the restaurant buffet car, with a kitchen capable of serving a large number of full meals, a small buffet counter for light snacks, and an adjoining saloon with 23 seats where passengers buying snacks at the buffet counter could sit without the necessity to carry food back to their own seats which might be at the far end of the train. Normally this type of car is paired at the kitchen end with either an unclassed dining saloon or an open first which is available to all passengers while they are having a meal. It means that a wide variety of meals and refreshments can be served, although inevitably while a full meal is in progress it might be necessary for the bar itself to be shut because of staff shortages or if a large number of diners require a set meal at the one sitting.

Propane gas was eventually standardised for cooking on all BR catering vehicles except BR's original full kitchen cars which had anthracite electric equipment as on latter day LNER catering vehicles.

BR also introduced two other types of catering vehicle not seen in quite the same form before. One was a miniature buffet with a bar counter taking the space that would otherwise be occupied by two bays of seats in an open second type of coach. The buffet has a Still for hot drinks and also serves a limited range of alcoholic drinks, and sandwiches, cakes, pies, crisps and confectionery, etc. They are often used on cross-country services where a full buffet or restaurant car would not be justified, and are sometimes operated by one man.

The other type of catering vehicle to make use of modern methods is the griddle car, fitted with a small central kitchen and buffet counter, which as its name implies is equipped with a griddle for the quick cooking of grill-type meals. At one end, the prototype griddle cars of the early 1960s included a lounge bar with curved longitudinal seats and the other had seats and tables for 12 passengers to eat hot snacks. Griddles also replaced conventional kitchen equipment on some Southern electric kitchen cars on the Portsmouth line and were adopted for the buffet cars in new express electric multiple-unit trains for both the Southern Region Sussex coast routes and the Eastern Region's Clacton service during the 1960s. With economies and cutbacks because of mounting losses on catering services the variety of fare offered on some of these buffets, particularly the range of hot snacks, was decidedly limited, sometimes being confined to toasted sandwiches, although supplemented by such convenience food as hamburgers available in a variety of themes combined with cheese or egg. Moreover, at the

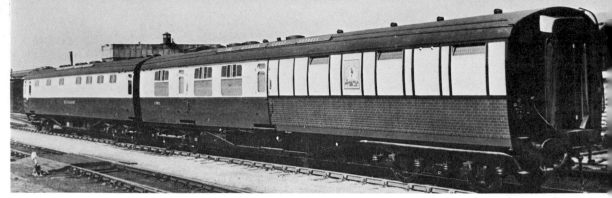

same time Pullmans on Southern Region services were well on the way out. The Pullman Car Company itself had been absorbed into the British Railways organisation so that although Pullman cars and staff continued to sport Pullman insignia they were nevertheless part of the British Railways network which ran and staffed all the other trains. It was therefore inevitable that Southern Region services, which in reality were little more than outer suburban in nature, would lose their Pullmans sooner or later. After all if Pullmans ran to Brighton, Eastbourne and Hastings why not Southend, Clacton, Bedford, Bletchley or Oxford? At first it was touch and go whether the replacement electric trains for the Southern's South Coast express services would have refreshments at all, but eventually they were provided with griddle buffets and the Pullmans were phased out.

This period also marked the beginning of the change not only to convenience food but also to packaging improvements and such less desirable aspects as cardboard or plastic cups, cardboard plates and plastic forks, spoons and knives. Most of the smaller items such as pies, cakes, etc sold in buffet cars are now prepacked and bought in bulk, but sandwiches are generally freshly made on the car, often to order but sometimes in batches in anticipation of a quick demand and always immediately wrapped in plastic film to maintain freshness.

Top: One of the Southern Region two-coach tavern dining sets built in 1949, finished externally in crimson lake and cream livery but with the tavern end picked out as brickwork with timber and whitewash upper panels. The taverns were named; this one was *The White Horse.* (*British Railways, SR*).

Centre right upper: The cocktail bar in one of the 1949 tavern cars. (*Keystone Press Agency*).

Centre right lower: The awkwardly arranged first class dining area of the 1949 tavern sets. There were no windows in the sides of the coach other than the upper sliding window ventilators. (*Keystone Press Agency*).

Right: One of the self-service cafeteria cars of the mid-1950s, this one with a long serving area and limited seating capacity. Other types included a small service area and central bar-type tables.

CHAPTER SEVEN

HIGH SPEED MEALS

Until the late 1950s the pattern of British express train services had not changed radically in timing or frequency for many years. There were a few exceptions where specified trains limited in weight and accommodation were given exceptional timings but most of the longer distance journeys relied on two or three fairly heavy and moderately-timed expresses a day. Certainly this was the case between London and Scotland, North Wales and Penzance. Only the Southern, with its electrified routes, had introduced frequent regular interval services running at hourly patterns through the day, although on certain other routes departure times had been standardised even though they might not have operated every hour. The Northern and Midland industrial towns and cities of Liverpool, Manchester, Leeds, Bradford and Birmingham in contrast had always enjoyed fast frequent services, designed for the needs of businessmen, in both directions. Cardiff, Swansea and Tyneside were also fairly well served but the Cornish businessman from Truro, for example, could not have arrived at Paddington by the first train of the day until 14.50, only 40min before the last day train back at 15.30.

The British Railways modernisation plan of the mid-1950s introduced diesel and electric traction to many routes, bringing a change in operating philosophy as timetables were recast to allow more frequent, lighter and faster expresses, a move stepped up in the 1960s as steam was eliminated and more powerful locomotives entered traffic. Permitted speeds were also lifted as track was improved, first to 90mph then on selected sections to 100mph. Journey times were cut and on some routes sets of coaches could now make two or even three single trips a day. No longer, too, were sets of coaches necessarily confined to one route and one set of coaches might find itself working from Leeds to Kings Cross, then Kings Cross to Edinburgh.

Moreover, in 1966/7 the West Coast route from Euston was electrified to Birmingham, Liverpool and Manchester with locomotive haulage on all express services and with sustained 100mph running by trains at regular hourly intervals, and even half hourly on the Birmingham line, journey times came down to 1hr 35min between Euston and Birmingham, 2hr 35min to Manchester, and 2hr 40min to Liverpool. With times like this the concept of train catering and staffing of catering cars had to be rethought, partly because coaching sets were in service for far longer during each working day than could be worked by crews and because a large number of passengers were likely to require snack meals in a short period. Even where multi-course main meals were still served it would not always be possible to do more than one sitting. Thus on some services, particularly on the Birmingham route, main courses consist of grill or griddle dishes.

Surprisingly in 1966 as part of the new electric services between Euston, Liverpool and Manchester, Pullman trains were included in the timetable, on a route, moreover, where Pullmans had never operated in normal service before, and some years after the Pullman Car Company had ceased to exist. The Pullman cars, which were specially built for the service and first class only, were allocated to two workings, one an all-Pullman train, which made two daily return trips between Manchester and Euston, and the other a similar working between Liverpool and Euston, though with first class Pullmans and second class ordinary coaches. A limited number of meals were served from the Pullman kitchen into the adjacent ordinary open second class coach. The Pullman attendants were drawn from BR's regular railway dining car crews. At the time of their introduction the Pullman supplement of £1.5s.0d (£1.25) was charged on top of the ordinary first class fare, with meals in addition.

The Pullman cars for the Liverpool and Manchester services followed basically the then current BR standard all-steel coach styles but were fully air-conditioned with double-glazed windows containing venetian blinds between the panes, and a high standard of sound and heat insulation. The seats could be adjusted either to a slightly reclining position, or upright if preferred during meal service, and were arranged two-and-one on each

side of the off-centre passageway. What a contrast between these cars, which as it has turned out will be the last Pullmans to be built for British Rail, and the first Pullmans built 92 years before.

The Liverpool/Manchester Pullmans followed very much the style internally of new set formation diesel Pullman trains which had their own power cars rather than independent locomotive haulage, introduced in 1960. Two types of unit were provided, six-car first class only trains for the Midland Pullman service between St Pancras and Manchester, and eight-car formations including first and second class for Western Region services between Paddington and Birmingham and to Bristol. The power cars were streamlined and the trains were decked out in a new blue and white livery, instead of the then standard Pullman umber and cream, from which they were known as the Blue Pullmans. They were capable of 90mph running and by contrast to surviving steam-hauled expresses, and even the rather uninspiring diesel locomotives of the time, really looked like the trains of the future. The new diesel Pullmans brought a new standard of accommodation, particularly on the Western Region where second class passengers paid no more than 5s (25p) on top of the ordinary fare from Paddington to Bristol. This was rail travel at its very best.

For 100 years the history of rail catering and accommodation standards has been inextricably bound up in one way or another with Pullmans even though Pullmans were confined to very few routes. Their influence was in competition which led other railways to raise standards, yet there has always been sales resistance to the payment of Pullman supplements.

The Pullman Car Company was taken over as a subsidiary company by the British Transport Commission in 1954 with an agreement that any future luxury supplement trains would run under the Pullman banner, like the Blue Pullmans. This proved not to be entirely practicable since railway dining car crews felt that they could provide similar service. The Midland Pullman was staffed by London Midland rather than Pullman men.

Top: Last of the Pullmans, the Euston–Manchester Pullman which entered service in 1966; all the cars had full sound insulation and air conditioning. (*London Midland Region, BR*).

Above: Standards and service on the Manchester Pullman reached the highest levels of railway catering and could match that of any comparable hotel. Venetian blinds between the panes of the double glazed windows were a feature of these mid-1960s Pullman sets. (*London Midland Region, BR*).

It was perhaps inevitable that if there was to be an expansion of Pullman-type trains, particularly on business services, which could expect a good proportion of expense account passengers prepared to pay more for that extra service, then Pullman operation would have to be conducted entirely as part of the British Rail Catering organisation. As a result the Pullman Car Company was totally merged into British Transport Hotels, which controlled the catering activities on the trains, from January 1963. But apart from the Liverpool and Manchester Pullmans of 1966 no other new Pullman services were started.

Not all Pullmans ran at times suitable for business travel and many other expresses of the 1960s were by then running at speeds of up to 90mph, or 100mph on the East and West Coast main lines. Even the West of England was at long last recognised as having business potential with new morning expresses to London and evening trains back between Plymouth and Paddington. In

1972 the service to the far west from Paddington was recast completely on an hourly basis, at least as far as Exeter or Newton Abbot, after which some trains terminated at Paignton while others ran to Plymouth or Penzance. More important though was the bold step of extending the Golden Hind express which had formed the early morning departure from Plymouth to London at 7.00, returning at 17.30, to and from Penzance, with little alteration of its timing between Plymouth and London. This meant the remarkably early start of around 5.00 from Penzance and with an arrival at Paddington at 10.38 at long last gave Cornish businessmen a morning service to London allowing around six hours in the capital for meetings or calls before leaving Paddington at 17.30 and arriving back at Penzance at nearly 23.00.

So far as train catering was concerned, the workings were re-organised so that restaurant cars on Penzance trains ran only between Paddington and Plymouth where the catering vehicles, usually comprising a buffet restaurant car coupled to an open first and one or two of the ordinary coaches were detached from down trains and attached to up trains. By this means the catering cars on several workings were able to do a full return journey plus another single journey between London and Plymouth.

The new 100mph services on East and West Coast main lines attracted far more than businessmen, for the speed and frequency of services brought a considerable increase in second class travel right through the day, and rather than expand the development of selected expresses with luxury Pullman accommodation, by the end of the 1960s BR clearly envisaged a raising of standards in ordinary stock to match those of the air-conditioned cars of the diesel Blue Pullmans and LMR electric Liverpool/Manchester Pullmans. Moreover, the improvement was to be for both first and second class passengers. Pullman services clearly did not have a long term future and one by one have been withdrawn.

From 1971 air-conditioned coaches, with double-glazing and good sound and heat insulation, were beginning to appear on principal express services. One feature, the gradual trend towards open saloon accommodation in both second and first class, was not to everyone's liking but this time history did not repeat itself by comparison with a century earlier, when objections forced the Midland Railway to abandon its open saloon coaches in its 1874 Pullman train, because open accommodation is now firmly part of the British travel scene. Economics play a large part for it is essential that second class vehicles should carry 64 passengers in the older standard 65ft stock and 72 passengers in the latest BR Mark III coaches which are 75ft in length. In side corridor vehicles this would entail seating eight to a compartment and it is not practical to include tables, but in open saloon coaches seats can be arranged in pairs at tables for four on each side of the central passageway. The main disadvantage is that noisy passengers in one part of a coach can annoy all the passengers in the vehicle, while one fresh air fiend who insists on the window being open can produce a howling gale throughout the coach. However, modern air-conditioned stock, with fixed windows, except in doors, overcomes the latter problem, and even interior noise tends to be deadened by the sound insulation in modern vehicles.

With the need to keep train weight to a minimum in order to achieve high speeds without a super abundance of power, BR today does not feel justified in keeping coaches solely for dining seats and on several services with limited formation trains there is a growing tendency for part of the first class accommodation to serve as restaurant seats. This means that first class passengers requiring meals can book a seat and travel all the way in the restaurant car. Shades of Midland practice again! Seats not taken in this way may then be left 'fluid' for first or second class passengers in other parts of the train who require

meals. Sometimes the first class accommodation is fairly well booked and the seats in the restaurant buffet car itself, normally used by passengers requiring light refreshments, may need to be used for the service of full meals. This could be potentially embarrassing on an otherwise fully air-conditioned train since apart from the Manchester Pullman catering vehicles none of the restaurant buffets or other vehicles with kitchens built in the 1950s and 1960s and in current use on many locomotive-hauled trains have air-conditioning.

The next stage in the travel revolution was introduced in 1976 when BR entered the ultra high-speed era with the new diesel-powered 'High Speed Trains' (HSTs) now known as Inter-City 125 trains from their ability to run at sustained top speeds of 125mph on suitable sections of line. They first appeared on Paddington–Bristol/South Wales services and two years later started running on the East Coast main line between Kings Cross and Edinburgh. Gradually they will also be introduced to other non-electrified trunk routes. In concept the Inter-City 125 units owe something to the 1960s diesel Blue Pullmans for they are fixed formation units with a streamlined power car at each end, although in this case without passenger accommodation. Intermediate coaches vary in composition according to route, but are made up entirely of the latest British Railways Mark III 75ft long air-conditioned coaches. There the resemblance with the Pullmans ends, for the Inter-City 125 trains include both first and second class accommodation and restaurant and buffet facilities, but above all there is no supplement to pay. They thus bring speed and high standards of passenger comfort to all. If there can be criticism it is that when fully loaded, for they are very popular trains, the second class looks really full. Moreover, because second class seats do not entirely match the window layout passengers in certain seats must perforce gaze on a blank wall instead of looking out through a window. So popular are these trains that on certain services additional trains have had

to be introduced into an already intensive timetable.

The new Inter-City 125 services, bringing the cities they join together that much closer in time, have also posed questions on future railway catering, for with Bath and the outskirts of Bristol no more than 1hr 10min away from London, with Cardiff and York just under and over 2hr respectively, and Edinburgh 4hr 50min from Kings Cross, it really becomes a case of fast service of meals and snacks. Moreover, with trains every half hour to Bristol, hourly to Cardiff, and two-hourly to Edinburgh, there are more than business expense-account passengers and holidaymakers to consider, for day trips are now possible between Glasgow or Edinburgh and London or vice-versa, and shopping trips to London are but an Inter-City 125 ride away from Bristol, South Wales or the West Riding. With the introduction of 125/150mph electric Advanced Passenger Trains on the West Coast route bringing Euston and Glasgow within four hours travelling time the same considerations will apply.

Thus Travellers-Fare, as the train and station catering division of British Transport Hotels is now known, has had to bear in mind wide-ranging markets in preparing new restaurant and buffet car designs. There is still a need for set meals on journeys of two hours or more, particularly at the top class end of the market. Equally, though, there is a demand for a grill or griddle service for quick meals or single courses, which on some routes can be provided as the main form of catering with waiter service, but which on others is organised on a self-service basis from a buffet counter, although meals are cooked to order.

Thus three different types of catering vehicle have been built for Inter-City 125 trains, a kitchen car without buffet counter but with 24 unclassed seats for dining purposes usually marshalled next to open first class vehicles, a buffet bar car with small kitchen and 35 second class seats, and a restaurant buffet bar car with a large kitchen but only 17 seats. The latter type can serve both main meals and hot snacks as well as the range of cold buffet counter items. The buffet car with small kitchen is not equipped to prepare a large number of table d'hôte meals at one sitting. Normally the restaurant-buffet car runs singly on shorter distance trains, but on the longer journeys there will usually be a kitchen diner at the first class end, and a kitchen-buffet bar car amidst the second class vehicles. Grills, griddle, hot plates and microwave ovens are used in varying combinations to prepare hot snacks to order, for the emphasis on Inter-City 125 buffets is very much on quick meals. Such snacks as egg, bacon and sausage, or a beefburger are served in plastic containers, rather like small boxes, which allow passengers to carry snacks easily to their own seats. Tea and coffee in self-service buffet cars has also become instant with plastic cups, pre-filled with powdered tea or coffee and milk and requiring only the addition of hot water. It is not to everyone's taste but from the Travellers-Fare point of view pre-packed tea and coffee has brought much stricter portion control and savings in cost. Moreover, with disposable cups, plates, cutlery etc there is little washing up to do.

Inter-City 125 trains have also reintroduced a feature of British train catering that has had a rather chequered career, the trolley service in which the buffet car steward takes a trolley equipped with a cash register, and supplied with tea, coffee, a selection of minerals, sandwiches, cakes, etc down the train. This has always been a controversial aspect of British railway operation largely because of the confined space in British coaches and by the fact that in a crowded train it is not possible for the steward to pass through if passengers are standing or passageways are blocked with luggage. On many trains buffet staff provide a train service of tea, coffee and sandwiches, carried by the stewards on a tray.

More than 1,000 British trains every day have refreshment facilities of one form or another, more than most of the trains with catering in mainland Western Europe put together. Yet with the exception of a few services most lose money, but are regarded by British Railways as an important passenger amenity which is subsidised from train fares. Restaurant cars never have been profitable and even in the 1890s the Great Western management was reluctant to introduce them because of that fact. Yet the British travelling public expects to be able to buy at least a cup of tea on a long distance train but does not think about how much it costs to provide it. A railway refreshment car really has a captive load of potential customers and because of that is under very close scrutiny in choice of fare offered, in presentation, and in price. Yet because of the peculiar circumstances of railway operation staff costs will be high and, moreover, since the kitchen is being whirled along day in day out at 100/125mph maintenance standards of the running gear must also be high for a small defect can put the car out of commission and mean that advertised catering services cannot be provided. The service of high speed meals must be just as safe and reliable as the high speed trains themselves.

CHAPTER EIGHT

INSIDE THE KITCHEN – AND OUT

Inevitably the kitchen and its equipment form the focal point of railway catering. Whether it has no more than a hot plate and grill, as in some of the smaller pantry buffets of the past, or a full range of cooking equipment capable of handling meals for 100 or more passengers at one time, smooth operation is only achieved if the design of the car is right, its equipment reliable and with staff working together as a team. There is no doubt that restaurant car chefs achieve high standards in kitchens so small that no land-based chef in a restaurant serving an equivalent number of meals at one and the same time would be called to work in. Indeed, the average railway kitchen in one of today's buffet restaurant cars is only little larger than those in modern three-bedroomed semi-detached houses, measuring something like 12–15ft in length by 6ft across. Yet in that area must be included all the essentials of the cooking equipment, for example roasting and steam ovens, grill, hot plates, hot cupboards, hot water urn, serving counters, sinks and drainers. Apart from

Interior of a British Railways full kitchen car of the early 1950s with anthracite electric cooking, the main stoves of which are seen in the background. This type of car was intended for the service of a large number of set menu meals at one sitting. (*London Midland Region, BR*).

that there are shelves for storage of pots and pans and other kitchen utensils, and some cars from the 1930s had refrigerators. If they did not have a refrigerator they usually had a cold cupboard surrounded by an ice box using wet ice. Today refrigerators and freezers are standard items.

The pantry is next to the kitchen, sometimes linked with a serving hatch, and usually provided with a Still's tea and coffee set and milk urn, operated by the attendants themselves. The pantry includes a bottle store for wines and spirits etc and dry store for all the kitchen car dry food, for example flour and fat for making pastry.

The first kitchens of a century ago were equipped with solid fuel stoves with a chimney to lead the smoke out through the car roof, but, without the benefit of proper draughting to ensure that the smoke went up the chimney, there was always a risk that outside air movement as the train was in motion, particularly with air turbulence in tunnels, would cause a downdraught which would envelop the kitchen in smoke and give the food a certain sooty flavour. Oil gas, which was coming into general use for lighting during the 1880s, was soon found to be a suitable alternative and most cars from then on were equipped for gas cooking. As we have seen, though, the gas storage tanks under the coach were a potential danger in an accident, for they were highly inflammable.

It was to overcome this objection that Gresley on the Great Northern and later LNER opted for electric cooking. The capacity of the system was limited, even though high capacity generators driven from the coach axles, and supplementing the batteries, powered the kitchen equipment when the train was on the move. It also meant that the LNER had to instal a network of power lines for electric kitchens at principal stations and sidings where trains terminated or stood waiting to start their journey. Moreover cars with electric kitchens could not work away from routes not equipped with land-line connections at main stations, a further limit on flexibility. As a result, Gresley went back to solid fuel from the late 1930s for certain cars, supplemented by a limited amount of electric equipment which was well within the capacity of the car's generator and battery. This time anthracite stoves had fan-assisted forced draught, and could be controlled much more readily than the original solid fuel stoves. The only problem was that chefs and their assistants had to learn to become firemen because the performance of the stove could be affected by the way in which the stove was fuelled.

The LMS and Great Western meanwhile continued to use oil gas. By the 1950s, liquid bottled gas was becoming available, a much safer product and available in steel containers of varying sizes and all transportable and fairly easily handled. The gas containers out-lasted a normal day's work and could be changed over for full bottles during normal servicing. Propane gas is now the standard fuel on all locomotive-hauled catering vehicles on BR at the time of writing. The only exceptions are on the London Midland Manchester Pullman kitchens, which use propane gas for the main ovens and range, but have some of the smaller grills, hot cupboard and Stills tea/coffee unit electrically powered off the train heating/air-conditioning electricity supply fed from the electric locomotive. Southern electric services including the Brighton Belle and other electric Pullmans of the 1930s were fitted with electric kitchen equipment from the start, a system which continues today on Southern electric services.

Electric cooking is also used on the new Inter-City 125 units, even though they are diesel-powered, but the motorcoaches have auxiliary generators supplying electric power through the train for air-conditioning and heating. The

The latest catering vehicles on BR Inter-City 125 trains include microwave ovens and all-electric equipment for grills, hot plates, griddles, etc. Beneath the microwave ovens seen at the far end are a refrigerator and freezer. (*British Railways Board*).

kitchens of Inter-City 125 restaurant cars are designed very much around modern catering trends and included in their principal equipment are microwave ovens. Microwave cookery has brought many new techniques, not least the remarkable speed at which cooking takes place. Certain grill items taking say 10–15min normally can be cooked in about one minute, baked dishes taking $\frac{1}{2}$hr to 1hr in a conventional oven can be dealt with in two or three minutes and even roast joints can be thoroughly cooked in a microwave oven in about 15min. Some items are cooked partially in a microwave oven and finished by conventional grill or griddle, since a microwave oven will not give a crisp brown finish to meat or pastry. Chefs on Inter-City 125 trains have thus had to learn new techniques to make the best use of their equipment. They have also had to overcome train effects with which they have not had to deal before, for example the higher speeds on certain curved sections where centrifugal force plays tricks on eggs newly broken on to a griddle to make them long and thin instead of broadly circular!

Microwave techniques on the latest Inter-City 125 trains and the general introduction of intensive stock use during the last decade have inevitably brought changes in kitchen practice. For many years the catering services of the railways had depots placed at strategic points, particularly at starting stations as at Kings Cross, Euston, Paddington etc, where a certain amount of food preparation and cooking was carried out to save time on trains. For example, large quantities of soup were prepared at the depot during the morning for transfer in containers to be finished off in restaurant car kitchens of trains starting journeys in mid-morning ready for lunch. Similarly joints would be partially or fully cooked in the depot and transferred to the car at the last minute, either for finishing or keeping hot ready for service soon after departure. By this means gas supplies of gas-equipped cars could be conserved, while electrically-powered cars, even while on land-line, could concentrate on other things such as cooking of vegetables. On some cars, because of journey times it was possible to cook joints totally on board. During recent years cooking and initial preparation at depots has now ceased, and nearly all cooking is now done in the cars themselves, largely because of a decline in the number of main meals served, particularly at lunch, and the impracticality of pre-cooking snack meals. Thus where joints are required on conventional cars they will often be cooked during a previous trip. For example, the preparation of dinner on trains leaving London in the late afternoon and early evening may be started on the previous up service to London during mid-afternoon. Sometimes this entails co-ordination between two crews where one crew relieves another on arrival in London, with the first crew say preparing the joint and starting to cook it, ready to be taken over by the second crew on the departing train. With microwave ovens, though, this is not necessary on Inter-City 125 trains.

The organisation behind the operation of railway catering cars is immense. Menus for main meals and the types of snack and buffet services to be provided on different trains are now determined at Travellers-Fare headquarters in London, in conjunction with the British Rail regions which have the say on the sort of service they require as part of the whole Inter-City travel package. As such, BR covers the loss on rail catering as part of the price in attracting business to Inter-City services.

At various times there has been central or more localised ordering from approved suppliers but restaurant car crews are basically responsible for ordering stock from the depots for their own car covering the menu of the day. Regular crews soon learn the level of business on specific services but obviously they will need to keep abreast of external factors that are likely to influence traffic, for example major exhibitions in London or other provincial centres, and, if possible, such last minute effects as fog or strikes on airlines which might mean a sudden influx of passengers, for example, on Anglo-Scottish services because flights are grounded. Stock supplied to each car is charged to that car and has to be accounted for by the receipts from it. Particular attention is naturally paid to bonded stock, that is cigarettes, wine, beers and spirits. Spirits and sherries are usually supplied in measures as bottled miniatures, while beer is invariably available canned rather than bottled. This has saved double-handling of beer bottles which had to be returned and credited. Inter-City 125 trains have draught beer available, the lack of which was a source of comment for many years, yet was a facility introduced on some of the privately-run tourist steam railways during the last decade.

The restaurant car crew is also responsible for the car's linen, for soiled tablecloths must be despatched to the depot, and thence to the laundry, at the end of each trip and clean supplies requisitioned to top up the car's allocation. All this has to be accounted for. Also at the end of each trip the crew has a vast amount of refuse to dispose of, including kitchen waste, used cans and cartons, broken glasses and crockery, and the like. All this accumulates during the journey and must be stored somewhere in the car. With short platform turnrounds it also means quick unloading of rubbish on arrival and restocking with fresh food, plastic cups, plates, cutlery and other containers. There is no doubt that the revolution in disposable containers has greatly eased the work of washing up, but waiter-served set meals still use conventional crockery and cutlery. Between the two wars the railways prided themselves on their standard of equipment with high quality heavy silver cutlery, linen napkins and tablecloths and quality crockery, which with detail changes, for example in lighter modern cutlery and paper napkins, continues today.

CHAPTER NINE

TAKE YOUR SEATS

There has always been a certain mystique about restaurant car practices, some of the secrets of which can be spotted by regular travellers. Apart from trains where meals were served at the passenger's seat, as on some LMS services or on Pullmans, the conductor or chief steward would need to know how many passengers he could expect through the train for each sitting. Thus soon after starting on trains leaving London, or the last major picking up point before lunch (or dinner), a steward would walk down the train looking in at each compartment to ask passengers if they required lunch and which sitting they wished to take. Usually a card was given to the passenger showing the sitting for which he was booked. About 20min before the meal was ready for service a steward again walked the train calling 'seats for first lunch'; passengers walked through the train taking seats in the diner as directed by the steward there or in accordance with seat numbers on the reservation card. When everyone was seated, one steward as wine waiter would pass down the car taking orders for drinks, but without an individual order pad how was each passenger's order noted? It was usually a simple affair with a quick sketch of the table plan of the car often on a scrap of paper, with stewards having their own shorthand system to note the requirements for each table. Once drinks were out of the way service of lunch began in earnest.

Traditionally main meals were and still are by silver service, that is by individual service from silver trays to the plate in front of the passenger to each passenger's own requirements. Thus one attendant would lead with fish or slices of joint or chicken portions, closely followed by other attendants serving vegetables. The essential feature of this service was that the empty plates in front of the passengers had to be warm and soon followed by the attendants serving the food. Any delay and the meal would be spoiled by being lukewarm.

If alternatives to soup were available, for example hors d'oeuvres, or in more recent years fruit juice — a post second world war phenomenon — the steward carrying a pile of warm soup plates would ask each passenger if he was taking soup, in which case a plate was placed in front of him ready for a second steward following with the tureen of soup. Meanwhile another steward would have served rolls, bread, or Ryvita and butter. Passengers taking the alternative course would be left without a plate so that when, say egg mayonnaise, arrived, already served on plates in the kitchen, the steward would know by the absence of a soup plate that the passenger was almost certainly taking the alternative choice.

For many years a fish course was served in four-course menus, and is included today on certain trains, and as an alternative to the meat entrée on three-course menus. The independent fish course has had a chequered career, disappearing for a time. Yet on dining cars in the 1960s we find a note on the menu, 'On Fridays an additional portion of fish will be served on request in lieu of the meat course'. Indeed religious observance has had to be borne in mind in preparation of menus, and roast pork, for example, has not featured quite as much as lamb, beef or chicken.

In recent years the sweet course has tended to be the somewhat uninspiring fruit salad with cream or ice cream, rather than hot puddings so beloved by our grandparents. Sometimes, though, the sweet consists of a fruit flan or pie, trifle or creme caramel. In a three- or four-course menu cheese and biscuits is an alternative to the sweet course, but at various times it could be had as an optional extra, and on today's gold star menus is included automatically as the fourth course, although such savouries as Welsh rarebit and mushrooms on toast are available as alternatives. Coffee service today on the gold star menu is included in the inclusive price based on which main course is taken, with up to two cups being served; normally it is charged as an extra on a per cup basis.

Over the years there have been many variations from one railway to another in service details, even though menu choices have not varied widely. On Great Western cars for example cheese and biscuits was usually accompanied by celery or watercress, while on some other lines it was plain cheese and biscuits and nothing else. At breakfast, the marmalade jar and the butter dish, with about $\frac{1}{4}$lb of butter, certainly looked less mean than individual portions spooned into a dish or butter cut into cubes or rolled, or today's individually wrapped butter portions and tiny pre-packed plastic pots of marmalade, often infuriatingly defying attempts to open them. In the 1930s despite the rising popularity of cereals for the domestic market, they had not penetrated dining cars, where breakfast nearly always began with porridge and cream.

Variations in presentation certainly gave some services a distinctive character. Most main meals were served on a fairly ordered basis with a prescribed menu, but some cross-country trains and, particularly, those running in the Scottish Highlands, never seem to have had quite the formality found elsewhere on BR, perhaps because their services have been more in the nature of à la carte menus served to a relatively small number of passengers so that the chef could spend more time on each order.

At one time before the general introduction of buffet cars with bar counters, morning coffee was served as a set item table d'hôte style with passengers called to the dining car just as for a full meal. Usually it consisted of coffee and biscuits, which on the Great Western were always Huntley & Palmers – who else since the GWR practically ran past that firm's front door at Reading? Indeed many of the railways built up a reputation for proprietary brands supplied specially packed for the particular railway. Half bottles of wine are sold at wine stores but for many years quarter bottles were available on Pullman cars. Each of the four group railways and Pullman prided themselves on their wine cellars and their buyers travelled round the great wine houses of Europe and the Empire to obtain the finest sherries, wines and spirits. Today British Transport Hotels maintains that same high standard, but the bottles are now metric.

Today more types of catering are generally available on BR trains than before. There is the all-purpose self-service buffet, which on some routes can serve hot snacks to order at the bar counter, and three types of waiter service menu – the Inter-City Grill, usually consisting of a two course meal for lunch, dinner or other times, the traditional three-course table d'hote service now known as the Main Line Menu and available at breakfast, lunch and dinner on most routes; finally, on selected business services, for breakfast and dinner the Gold Star Menu combines more courses, larger portions and includes more expensive foods, as for example at dinner, soup with fresh cream, prawn cocktail, and salmon.

The accompanying table and sample menus show the variations over the years, and prices must inevitably be compared with those in comparable restaurants on terra firma. But Travellers-Fare operations are run on a totally different basis. A restaurant on the ground, if indeed it served a set lunch at all, would certainly have staff on duty only for the main lunch period and then again for

Comparison of restaurant car prices

Date	Full Breakfast	Lunch	Dinner	Coffee (cup) with meal
1898		2s 0d*	3s 6d†	4d
1930s	3s 6d	2s 6d 3s 6d‡	5s 0d§	4d
1960	7s 6d	11s 0d§	12s 0d§	10d
1978	£2.45 (£2 9s 0d)	**	††	26p (5s 2½d)

* – 3rd class 4 courses GNR   † – 1st class 6 courses GNR
‡ – 5 courses   § – 4 courses
** 3 courses £3.35–£3.95 (£3 7s 0d–£3 19s 0d)
†† – 4 courses plus coffee Gold Star menu £4.95–£5.25 (£4 19s 0d–£5 5s 0d)

Above: Table showing comparison of meal prices over the last 80 years.

Right: One of today's BR 'Main Line' menus offered on many Inter-City long distance services.

Price of meal is governed by choice of Main Dish.
Prices include VAT, not service.

Spring Vegetable Soup
Selection of Chilled Fruit Juices
Grapefruit and Mandarin Cocktail

Roast Chicken, Bread Sauce   £4·40
Home-made Steak, Kidney and Mushroom Pie   £3·95
Fillet of Cod Mornay   £3·35
Cold Tongue, Ham and Salad   £3·35
Sliced Beans, Garden Peas
Roast and Boiled Potatoes

Chocolate Trifle
Cheese Board, Salad

Coffee Service   26p
Pot of Freshly Brewed Tea   26p

PLEASE ASK FOR A BILL AND RETAIN IT.

CHILDREN WELCOME You can take advantage of these special prices when children join you for a meal :–
Under 3 years – free; aged 3 and under 11 years – half price.

This menu is subject to alteration without notice.
*Cheques must be accompanied by a cheque card.
Please make cheques payable to "British Rail".
Diners are requested to refrain from smoking immediately prior to and during the course of the meal.
In case of difficulty, please call for the Chief Steward. Comments will be welcomed by the Managing Director, Travellers-Fare, St. Pancras Chambers, London, N.W.1 2TU.

Travellers·Fare

the preparation and service of dinner in the evening; on a restaurant car, once staff are on duty they cannot be booked off when the meal has ended until the train or restaurant car has reached its destination, and they must be paid for the hours during which they are at work. Some restaurant cars do not work right through with the main part of the train and might be scheduled to be detached intermediately. The present day arrangements on Paddington–Penzance trains have already been noted, though these will change with the introduction of Inter-City 125 units. In the Scottish Highlands for many years some restaurant cars workings appeared to terminate at stations in the middle of wild moorland or mountains, as for example Achnasheen on the Kyle line, and The Mound Junction or Helmsdale on the line from Inverness to the far north. With only two or three trains a day it was an arrangement to allow the car to cover two services in opposite directions and to enable the crew to do a return trip in a day not otherwise possible had the car gone right through with the main part of the train. Restaurant car staff sometimes work long hours, even today on certain routes, and particularly on charter trains, but on services where they would be on a roster calling for a 12hr day they work fewer days. Until the second world war restaurant car staff usually worked a 120hr fortnight but hours have been reduced to a 40hr basic week.

Clearly restaurant car operation is a serious business requiring a high calibre of staff to attain the standards of service essential for its success, and integrity, for in any business of this type there will be opportunities for staff to stray on to the wrong side of the law as for example the crew who ran their own coffee shop with their own supplies

within the buffet car, and pocketed the proceeds, found to their cost.

Yet there is a lighter and more human side to restaurant car life, as for example the dog waiting by the Somerset & Dorset line each day for a bone to be thrown from the kitchen of the Pines Express at just the right spot as it passed. The Great Western signalman who was just walking up the signalbox steps when a plateful of bones, heads and skin from whatever had been the fish course on a passing train met him square in the face, was, though, less pleased. Instructions went forth from Paddington the very next day forbidding the disposal of kitchen waste out of restaurant car windows as it was unhygenic, not to say off-putting to lineside staff!

In years past recruitment of restaurant car staff was either from juniors employed as pantry boys who worked their way up through the ranks, or, in the 1920s particularly, from men who had been in service in large houses in pre-first world war days, as the employment of servants and domestic staff declined. Today there is no one source of staff for restaurant cars, and new staff undergo special courses in training cars. Like many industries, in pre-second world war days staff tended to remain in jobs much longer than they do today and many of the older hands worked their way up, spending all their working life on restaurant cars. Today staff turnover is in the order of 25 per cent and with complex staff rostering means that teams do not always work together fully for very long.

Some trains, particularly those starting in the mornings from the provinces, are worked by regular crews and even today some of the staff have been many years in restaurant car service. Sometimes a rapport is often built up between staff and regular business travellers and while it is not always practicable for the chief steward to greet a customer with 'your usual table sir?' some of the passenger's likes and dislikes will be in mind during meal service, in much the same way that attention is given by a head waiter to a valued client at a favourite restaurant.

Travellers-Fare policy on food today is to use as much fresh food as possible, particularly meat, although a certain amount of frozen vegetables are used and some convenience foods in buffet cars. Home-made steak, kidney and mushroom pie, perhaps, is a slight misnomer for it is freshly made in the kitchen of the restaurant car, although chefs have a choice of using proprietary pastry mix or of making their own. The frozen complete main meals of the 1950s cafeteria cars have no place in today's BR menus.

In this study of railway catering over 100 years we have not looked at special trains or special events, but over the years railway dining cars have been included in many charter specials, often calling for a 16hr day – or more – ranging from football excursions, working men's outings, to first class specials conveying visitors to a ship-launching, a royal wedding, and to the working of the royal train itself, where selected railway restaurant car chefs and stewards provide meals for the royal party and attendants.

It may come as a surprise to learn that Travellers-Fare is now the only national caterer whose restaurants and buffets can be seen in so many widely scattered parts of the country. Certainly there are now few national chains of teashops across the country as there used to be, although some hotel groups with catering contracts on motorways and principal trunk roads are widely represented but not to the same extent as Travellers-Fare. As such rail catering is very much in the public eye and since its customers are very much a captive audience, isolated cases of indifferent service, staff rudeness or poor food reflects on the entire system. If passengers are dissatisfied with an in-town restaurant they can always go elsewhere next time but not so on a train. One unfortunate incident in a buffet car will be blamed on the entire railway system and the passenger will probably go by car or fly next time. Railway catering never was perfect, nor is it ever likely to be, but then someone will always find fault in public services.

It is around a century since George Mortimer Pullman set out to raise standards of passenger travel; he would have been proud of today's BR air-conditioned Inter-City 125 expresses, but it has taken 100 years of technological development and economic uncertainties to get where we are. What will happen in the next 100 years is anybody's guess but conventional railways have decided potential for still higher speeds, even if passenger amenities have virtually reached the limit of their development. As journey times decrease so will the demand for main meals but with the British love of eating between meals and tea-breaks the travelling public of the future will not willingly be parted from somewhere to eat and drink, even for the hour or two of most Inter-City journeys of the next decade.

'Cheers'; inside one of BR's latest Mark III air-conditioned coaches now used for restaurant service on a growing number of trains, although it will be several years before older stock is phased out on many routes. (*British Railways Board*).